***

Angels
and
Miracles

***

By the same author

An Angel At My Shoulder
Children and Angels

✳✳✳

Angels
and
Miracles

✳✳✳

Extraordinary Stories that
Cannot be Easily Explained

by
Glennyce S. Eckersley

RIDER

LONDON • SYDNEY • AUCKLAND • JOHANNESBURG

First published in 1997

9 8

Copyright © Glennyce S. Eckersley 1997

The right of Glennyce S. Eckersley to be identified as the Author of
this work has been asserted by her in accordance with the Copyright,
Designs and Patents Act, 1988.

All rights reserved. No part of this publication may be reproduced,
stored in a retrieval system, or transmitted in any form or by any
means, electronic, mechanical, photocopying, recording or
otherwise, without the prior permission of the copyright owner.

First published in 1997 as *Out of the Blue* by Rider,
an imprint of Ebury Press, Random House,
20 Vauxhall Bridge Road, London SW1V 2SA
www.randomhouse.co.uk
Reissued by Rider as *Angels and Miracles* in 2001
www.rbooks.co.uk

Addresses for companies within
The Random House Group Limited can be found at:
www.randomhouse.co.uk/offices.htm

The Random House Group Limited Reg. No. 954009

Papers used by Rider Books are natural, recyclable products made
from wood grown in sustainable forests.

A CIP catalogue record for this book is available from the British
Library
ISBN 978-0-7126-1203-6

Typeset by SX Composing DTP, Rayleigh, Essex

Penguin Random House is committed to a sustainable future for
our business, our readers and our planet. This book is made from
Forest Stewardship Council® certified paper.

Printed and bound in Great Britain by Clays Ltd, St Ives plc

In memory of
Anne & William Thaw

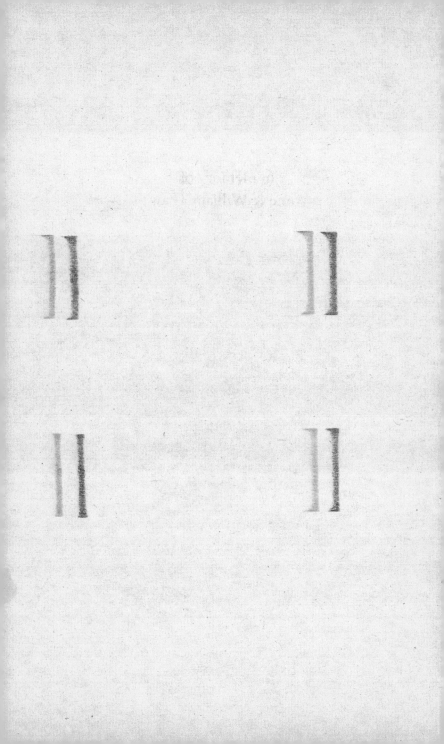

∗∗✳∗∗

Contents

Divine Providence does its work
out of sight and in ways
beyond comprehension,
for the reason that a person
may be able in freedom
to attribute that work either to
Providence or else to chance.

EMANUEL SWEDENBORG,
ARCANA CAELESTIA (HEAVENLY SECRETS)

$$ **\;**\;\text{\Large$*$}\;**\;** $$

Acknowledgements

I owe an immense debt of gratitude to several very special people. Firstly, a huge thank you to David Lomax, for his advice, considerable practical and moral support, patience and generosity. Thank you too to my editor, Judith Kendra, who always keeps smiling and helps me to keep my chin up through thick and thin. To Ian Carroll, for his expertise and willingness to help, I shall be forever grateful. I am also grateful to Jane Bullough for her cheerful assistance, and to Greta Woolf and Janice O'Gara for their considerable emotional support. My thanks also go to Ian Arnold, staff and students at the New Church College. Last, but by no means least, come gratitude and love to my long-suffering family, Ross, Gillian and Rachel.

I thank profusely the people without whom there would simply be no book for allowing me to tell their stories. They are: Helen Bailey, Rosie Ballantyne, Audrey Beecham, Connie Benetz, Janine Bentley, Gordon Bridges, Ann Bryant, Mary Bullough, Paul Bullough, Chris, Pamela & Roy Cuthbert, Mary,

Dennis & Julian Duckworth, Julie Fearnhead, Susan Gardiner, Kate Geers, Iris Gower, Daniel Green, Eva Barbara H, Barbara Hague, Alan Hardy, John Harley, Christopher Hasler, Clare Higgins, Jeannie & Paul Humphreys, David Krejza, Paul McNeilly, Diane Marsh, Pam & David Moffat, Pauline, Janice & Mark O'Gara, Sarah Pike, Yvonne Preston, Peter Radcliffe, Joanna & Ilani Redman, Kevin Roberts, Bethany Rowan, Mike Rowland, Karen Scott, Rene Seren-Dat, Amanda Smith, Steve, Jenny Sutton, Judith Varley, Jo Whittier-Marshall, Henrietta Walker, Beth and Michael Watson, Glenda Wiess, Megan Williams.

****

Introduction

This is a book about both coincidences and modern-day miracles, which are very closely interrelated. People talk more freely about coincidences, which happen frequently to many people and are more easily accepted. However, even these cases are not just a matter of *mere* coincidence, if we look at them more deeply. I prefer to see the meaning behind such happenings and, if we start to look at some of the issues which arise out of coincidences, they are often miraculous in their own way. This is what has brought about my own interest in coincidence, primarily from my own experience, because deeper meaning or spiritual significance seems to me to underlie these experiences. In writing this book I am very aware that I am not alone in this — many others have felt their lives touched by this phenomenon — but I thought it might be helpful to begin by relating a series of coincidences that linked several people and events surrounding my last book, which dramatically illustrates how mysterious and life-changing these events can be.

The first coincidence, although not spectacular in itself, set off a cluster of them and occurred when Robert Copeland, a television producer, was making a video about angels, immediately prior to my publication date. One day, dashing through a bookshop on his way to catch a train, he spied out of the corner of his eye a box with the lid lifted just enough to reveal the title of the book on its bright blue cover. This was my book, *An Angel at my Shoulder*. Intrigued, he bought a copy and ran with it to the train. Deciding he wanted to include several stories from it in his video he contacted me and it was arranged that contributors would be filmed relating their stories.

One young woman, Karen Scott, was very keen to help but had just that very week started a course at college. How on earth, she reasoned, could she ask her lecturer for time off, even an extended lunch hour? However, Karen felt strongly that she should take part since her story was important and could help and inspire others. Seizing courage with both hands she explained to her lecturer the dilemma facing her and asked if she would be lenient should Karen be slightly late back at college after the lunch break. Both she and the lecturer however were amazed to find that they both had appointments to be filmed for the video that day and so Karen was allowed to keep the appointment with an easy mind.

This was only the first of many coincidences that

day. Robert and his cameraman, Tom, had arrived early and set up their equipment. Whilst waiting for our first interviewee, we chatted about angels. Robert told me that he had heard of the existence of a photograph, taken from a plane window, which when developed revealed an angel. It emerged that an Australian woman, a very nervous flyer, was terrified when the plane she was abroad flew into a storm and hit severe turbulence. Lightning added to the drama and the woman started to pray, feeling sure she would not survive the flight. She recalled afterwards specifically asking God for a guardian angel to help her through the storm. Despite her fear, she was fascinated by the drama being played out by nature outside the plane window and decided to take a photograph of the skyscape. Eventually the storm abated and they landed safely. When the film was developed and the photographs were viewed, this astonished woman discovered the figure of an angel on the photograph she had taken from the plane window. The angel was all light and calm in the midst of the stormy sky.

As a television producer, Robert was very keen to find a copy of this photograph to include in his angel video. The Australian woman had had three copies made to send to friends around the globe and Robert knew that there was a print somewhere in England. However, exhaustive research and inquiries had failed to unearth this print and he was very disappointed, especially as it had allegedly been verified by experts as genuine.

The first interviewee to arrive was Kate, nervous but ready to relate her angelic experience to the video camera. I settled down to watch as Tom arranged the lights and recording equipment. At this point, Kate turned to me and said, 'Before we start, I have something to show you.' She took an envelope from her handbag containing a letter from a friend in Australia and the very photograph we had just been discussing! The photograph, I can reveal, is spectacular and produces shivers down the spines of all who view it.

COINCIDENCES AND EVERYDAY MIRACLES

The extraordinary thing about these experiences is that they always arrive suddenly, out of the blue. There is a link between the colour blue and heaven. It is not surprising that over the centuries this colour in its many different hues has taken on associations with the afterlife, and is used for draping coffins or depicting the clothing of angels. Generally speaking, it reminds us of both divine eternity and human immortality. As we shall see, stories of coincidences and miracles can do the same.

The blue of the sky no longer has an automatic resonance with heaven, but many people are still searching for meaning and pattern. Putting together this book has shown me that not only are people searching but many are finding what they are looking for. Perhaps this is why I feel I am not just talking about coincidence in its commonest meaning of a throw-away event of little importance. When reading stories such as the ones included here it becomes easier to believe that everyday miracles are still very much part of our world. This is probably why coincidences are attracting so much interest and attention today. It looks as if they are not only widespread but perhaps becoming increasingly frequent.

Coincidences are something we all relate to – the 'mini-miracles' happening around us. Everyone has experienced coincidences, no matter how small, as they are part of the normal fabric of our daily lives. Most people have been in situations where, for example, they are thinking about a friend with whom they may have contact only sporadically and they receive a letter or phone call from them. You may hear a word or a piece of music for the first time and suddenly it seems to be everywhere at once. Then there is the widespread experience of bumping into people in unforeseen and highly unlikely circumstances, or meeting someone for the first time and finding there are extremely close connections between the two of you.

I believe that coincidences are modern mini-miracles because they almost always contain a spiritual element, either in the sense of revealing our own sensitivity and powers — listening to premonitions, 'inner voices', and telepathic communication — or a sense of visitation from another world or higher realm, in the form of answers to prayers, divine messages and angelic guidance.

Having looked in depth at other forms of spiritual experience for my last book, I have been very keenly aware that not everyone is privileged enough to see an angel or vision, or be involved in a spiritually uplifting near-death experience. Yet even when this is not obviously the case, coincidences often have a life-changing quality. Such events offer glimpses of hope and new possibilities which may transform depression and despair, inspiring people to move on in their lives, to make changes that help them fulfil their potential. Sometimes this happens simply through an unexpected meeting or reunion, sometimes through being rescued or saved from accident or certain death, as some of the stories in this book illustrate. Also included here are moving accounts of the effect of spiritual healing in its many forms, although this too is perhaps not as commonly experienced as we might wish, however accessible it may be today.

What underlies all these experiences, whether seemingly mundane or a full-blown miracle, is a sense of connection and unity. We realize that we are not alone in the world, no matter how lonely and abandoned we may sometimes feel. These unexpected meetings – help from a stranger, escape from certain death, glimpses of natural or heavenly beauty – show us that, after all, we live in a caring and compassionate universe. If we can learn to trust in life and in our own intuition and inner promptings, we can begin to live in harmony with the universe, which will bring us happiness and fulfilment.

SCIENTIFIC, PSYCHOLOGICAL AND SPIRITUAL EXPLANATIONS

These are obviously not new types of experience, even if there is a high level of interest in such events today. In fact, coincidences seem always to have been part of human experience, and there have been different ways of interpreting their significance through the ages. I have turned to some of these explanations throughout the book and I should like to refer briefly to them now in this introduction, beginning with modern science.

One of the things which has led me to investigate coincidences and to write this book is the number of coincidences surrounding my previous book, *An Angel at my Shoulder*. This illustrates a point made by one of the first historical figures who felt that coincidence merited scientific study. He was an Austrian biologist,

Paul Kammerer, who felt that the *clustering* of coincidences, as he termed it, was a natural phenomenon. He explained clustering as a 'run' of events or groups of people experiencing the same event. Kammerer's work early this century was primarily about recording and classifying this clustering, whereas psychologists such as Carl Jung later concentrated on the meaning and symbolism of coincidences. Carl Jung applied the word 'synchronicity' to the phenomenon of coincidence. In doing so, he was drawing attention to his strong belief in the significance of events which happen at the same time. Dreams were also a key element of Jung's work, and one classic example of their importance to the development of his theories and their link to reality in the life of one of his patients is included in my chapter on dreams in the well-known story of the scarab beetle. The fact that dreams play a prominent role in many stories may be because symbolism plays a large part not only in dreams generally but also in looking specifically at the meaning of some people's amazing coincidence experiences.

An interest in miracles, dreams, symbols and synchronicity links us not only with people all over the globe, of every race and creed, but also with ancient peoples who lived thousands of years ago and experienced the same phenomena. Jung researched ancient cultures and their mythologies to establish the identities of what he called 'archetypes', common features united in particular symbols or figures. He suggested as an explanation of these archetypes a collective unconscious to which we all have access. This differs from the idea of a personal unconscious which stores all our memories, because it includes other people and reinforces the belief that we are all linked together at a deeper level. The theory of the collective unconscious becomes significant when we are thinking about coincidences because here too we have some sense, however vague, of our ability to be connected with others, although perhaps in a way which we do not fully understand. Without this theory of the collective unconscious, it would be sometimes difficult to explain how a certain train of events for different individuals or even groups of people can be drawn together in a coincidental event.

This sense of being connected to people and things outside ourselves is probably the reason why coincidences have such an impact on us, especially since, today, isolation and separation are very much a part of the modern world. However, it was not always so. Peoples living thousands of miles apart, long before modern communications and technology, had almost identical symbols in their lives. Take the 'dream catcher', familiar to Aborigines and Native Americans. It is a round frame woven with threads in a 'spider's web' pattern and, in the case of Aborigines, often literally a spider's web lifted on to a wooden frame.

This device is placed behind your head whilst you sleep and will 'catch' your dream. The coincidence that native peoples living at opposite ends of the world should use the same unusual artefact can be seen as, at one level, an extraordinary sign of relationship or interconnection between them.

The 'dream catcher' is interesting not just because it provides a common link between cultures, but also because it can be seen as a type of mandala. These are ancient symbolic pictures, generally circular in shape, and elements of them can be found in many different traditions – even in some of the very latest geometric patterns discovered by chaos theory.

Chaos theory has developed over the last twenty or thirty years as a special field which straddles different scientific disciplines, starting with the work of Edward Lorenz on weather (a rich form of chaos, as we know only too well!) in the early sixties. It shows that forms and events which on the surface seem chaotic or meaningless reveal subtle patterns and purpose when studied more holistically. This new thinking has given the name 'fractals' to the forms of chaos, many of which we see in the forms and patterns of the natural world, such as the growth of a tree, or the movement of the water of a fast-flowing stream. Fractals were identified and named by the mathematician Benoit Mandelbrot, and could only be found after computers had reached modern levels of sophistication thanks to the silicon chip. They are thus miracles of both nature and science, revealing order in chaos, and mirroring the links of coincidence in our own apparently chaotic lives.

Basically, fractals are patterns in nature which when viewed on a small scale look exactly as they do on a larger scale. A small fraction of a leaf, for instance, mirrors the pattern of the leaf as a whole.

Chaos theory has emerged as scientists have learned to see patterns which are very subtle or complex, and the scientists' definition of chaos is of a non-linear phenomenon, literally something that does not travel in a straight line. This is why pictures of fractals (as on the cover of this book) inevitably involve curves and spirals. This seems to me to be a perfect parallel to the way in which coincidences emerge and make complex swirling patterns in our lives. These pictures are based on equations named after Mandelbrot, the Mandelbrot set, and today's computers allow pictures and shapes of a re-emerging pattern to be magnified thousands and millions of times. Another amazing thing is that fractals go on to infinity. These patterns, however, look strikingly like multi-coloured mandalas of the Native Americans while similar patterns can be found in art from different religious traditions, whether Christian, Islamic, Hindu or Buddhist.

If tribal wisdom, ancient art, nature, psychology, and the computer-generated pictures of today's mathematics all have a link, it begins to appear, therefore, that coincidences (and miracles) are not just about individual and personal consciousness but involve a higher order. Could consciousness really be shared by groups of people? Are we led providentially even though we have the free will to choose the path we take? I say this knowing full well that such terms as 'providence' and even 'free will' are normally associated with religion. Perhaps drawing together these different fields can add new dimensions to these traditional religious ideas and encourage us to build a stronger sense of something that unites us all.

As well as including many people's experiences in this book, I have sought to put forward pictures, analogies and theories which illustrate this interconnectedness of things on a non-material level, as is suggested by the concept of synchronicity. Seeing coincidence as meaningful involves us in accepting a sense of a greater whole, something which can bring together different parts of a system in harmony; as I have already mentioned, much modern-day thinking in this field links with ancient traditions. I hope you will feel as you read this book that our world is full of extraordinary interconnections, and see clear patterns emerging which stress the similarities between new and ancient beliefs and ways of life, between the traditional tribal wisdom and the cutting edge of today's scientific thinking.

✳✳✳ 1 ✳✳✳

Everyday Miracles

*'Not a whit, we defy augury; there's a special
providence in the fall of a sparrow. If it be now, 'tis
not to come; if it be not to come, it will be now; if it
be not now, yet it will come; the readiness is all.'*

WILLIAM SHAKESPEARE

I have already suggested that one of the most striking characteristics of coincidences is their universality. Sometimes they may be so remarkable as to defy belief. The coincidences in this chapter are of the everyday variety, things which could happen to us all, and indeed do. Most people have been in situations where they are thinking about a friend and then a letter arrives from them or they telephone. We may find ourselves singing absent-mindedly only to hear the same song broadcast on the radio minutes later. We may exclaim in slight surprise and immediately forget the incident but sometimes, even though the incident seems minor, it is so helpful to the people concerned that it makes a strong impact.

Sometimes an apparently simple, even banal, event such as finding a long-lost but much loved object can appear almost miraculous, as in the following heart-warming story.

Megan's father had smoked a pipe for as long as she could remember. This was not always a welcome activity and from time to time he would be banished to the garden when the smell of his tobacco became over-whelming. Taking his trusty silver pen-knife from his pocket, he would often scrape the bowl for hours, and this action was clearly therapeutic rather than func-tional.

The pen-knife was quite old and rather beautiful, distinctively patterned with flowers and leaves. Megan's son coveted this pen-knife greatly and felt most privileged when he reached his early teens and was occasionally allowed to whittle pieces of wood with it. Early in the summer of 1986, the entire family visited a country show in the Lake District, a pleasant event with something for everyone. Craft stalls and food tents were especially popular and it was inside the food tent that Megan heard her mother admonish her father for producing his knife and pipe. Placing them on the seat beside him, he had it in mind to eat lunch and then take a long stroll, during which he could puff away to his heart's content.

As the family piled into cars for the journey home, a cry of despair and disbelief went up. Megan's father had lost his pipe and pen-knife. Everyone searched the showground but to no avail. The refreshment tent had already been dismantled and no amount of looking produced the much-loved objects. The day was ruined for the whole family. Megan's father was terribly distressed, and Megan's son was also very sad for he had hoped that his grandfather might have eventually been persuaded to let him have the knife.

Years went by and the incident was forgotten. Megan's son left to go to university in Bath, where he was to study chemistry. He soon made new friends and the new-found independence was also appreciated, apart from the aspect which was its one drawback — money. His grant never seemed to last, and, like most of his friends, he was permanently penny-pinching.

Swiftly, he began to learn where to shop for bargains, and one day, on deciding that he really could use a new jacket, he was pointed in the direction of the nearest Oxfam shop by a friend. The shop was a revelation, full of interesting objects new and old and a wide range of clothes. Searching along the coat rack, he found a jacket that looked warm and reasonable and he tried it on. Looking in the shop mirror, he decided that it was perfect for his needs and that he would buy it. On impulse, he thrust his hands into the two deep pockets and, incredibly, pulled out his grandfather's pen-knife! To this day it is a mystery as to how it arrived in Bath.

EXTRAORDINARY MEETINGS AND REUNIONS

Some stories of coincidental meetings are startling when one considers the odds against this happening; some are full of humour, whilst others lead you to think only the hand of providence could have engineered such an incident. The next few stories contain all these elements.

Jenny was back in England after several years living in New Zealand. She had made arrangements to meet her sister at the busy London station from which they would travel west together to their parents' home. To add to Jenny's excitement, she was pregnant and was looking forward to chatting with her sister about the future. Arriving at the appointed spot at exactly the right time, Jenny was surprised to find no sign of her sister, who was usually very prompt. Time ticked by and Jenny became increasingly anxious. The time for the train to depart was fast approaching and she pondered on the dilemma facing her. Should she catch the train without her sister (trains were not very frequent and her parents would be expecting them) or should she let it go without her and wait to see if her sister would appear?

At this point, anxiety mounting, she began to feel nauseous and decided that she would get on the train. She walked along the train in search of an empty space, but it was quite full. Eventually, she came to a carriage with a few empty seats and thankfully sat down. A kindly-looking lady sitting opposite asked if she was all right, noticing how agitated she was, and Jenny told her of her problem. 'Don't worry,' she replied, 'she will be here any minute. I just sat next to her on the Tube. She told me she was meeting you and that her train had been delayed and she hoped you would not be too worried.'

When you think of all the people on all the Underground trains, packed like sardines, next to whom this lady could have sat, this was a spectacular coincidence. Sure enough, a minute later Jenny's sister appeared.

Christopher was attending an international seminar in Manchester. Among the participants was an ex-student of the college where the seminar was being held, visiting all the way from New Zealand. The seminar involved a full programme and was intellectually demanding, so a short break in the form of a free afternoon was welcome. Christopher had travelled to Manchester from the south-east coast of England and was reminiscing with the New Zealand visitor about the days when he had lived and worked in the Manchester area, some twenty-five years before. They decided to have a ride to the small Lancashire town and find the spot where Christopher had lived.

The town was busier and a good deal more built up than Christopher remembered, but he found the crescent of houses looking much the same. They got out of the car having parked outside the gate, and were talking about the days long ago and all that had happened in the interim. Suddenly, they became aware of a car pulling up behind them and a woman getting out. 'Do you intend being here some time?' she asked, obviously a resident. Apologizing, Christopher explained that he had lived in that house twenty-five years ago and was visiting for the first time since then. 'Are you the Reverend C. Hasler?' she asked. 'Indeed I am,' he replied. 'Splendid,' she said. 'I have some mail for you, recently arrived', and reaching into her handbag she pulled out a postcard addressed to him which had come only the day before!

It was hot and dusty as Sarah and her friends arrived at the jolly, bustling station to await a train to Bombay. One of the party was a medical student and their conversation must have made this obvious, for they were approached by a European man wearing a large hat as protection from the sun. Laughing, the man announced that he was also a kind of doctor. 'What kind?' he was asked. At this point, he removed his hat and everyone laughed as they recognized Dr Legge from *EastEnders*. They all enjoyed the joke and travelled to Bombay together. He was a friendly character and an interesting person. Whilst in Bombay, Sarah wrote a postcard to her friend at home in Liverpool, knowing she would be amused.

The friend was reading the postcard while walking down a street in Liverpool when she was stopped politely and asked the way to a certain store. It was none other than Dr Legge! Having finished filming an episode of *EastEnders*, he had just arrived in Liverpool to star in a play at the Everyman Theatre. Sarah's friend was struck dumb with surprise but when a second friend, having spied the actor, told him they were friends of the people he had met in India, it was his turn to be amazed.

Eventually Sarah arrived home from India and caught up with the news. Pondering the incident, she sat on the sofa watching TV when, to her surprise, she saw that Gary Bushell was hosting an interview with the very same Dr Legge. Sarah laughed out loud, at which point a friend joined her in the room and asked what she was finding so amusing. Taking a deep breath, Sarah was just about to relate the story when Dr Legge started to tell the series of coincidences to Gary Bushell. The whole thing felt very spooky indeed.

There was a final twist to the tale, so to speak, when Sarah discovered that some time previously she had shared a student house with the actor's son – another link in this chain of synchronicity for Sarah.

This next story did not happen to the woman telling it, but she witnessed the coincidence as it occurred. Here is her account:

It was a bitterly cold night, the Saturday before the Christmas of 1996. I was travelling on the Underground in London anxious to get home out of the cold and away from the Christmas crowds in central London. Lucky to find just one seat on the crowded train, I gratefully sat down. The young woman sitting next to me smiled and I thought how happy she looked, dressed for some special occasion. At the next station a huge tide of humanity flowed into the train, including one young man who looked anxious, pale and rather confused. Suddenly, he caught sight of the young woman sitting next to me and let out a whoop of delight. The lady responded by jumping up and hugging him warmly, clearly amazed to see him.

They were both Americans and by now so excited they were talking in very loud voices so the incredible story was heard by the entire carriage. What emerged was that they had been high school friends in a small town in Ohio, and had not seen each other since graduation some six years previously. He had gone to university in another state and she had travelled to Europe, eventually finding a job in London where she had been for the past four years. The young man had arrived from the States only the day before. He had stayed in a small hotel the previous night but was now

20

hopelessly lost. Clutching the piece of paper with the hotel's address on it, he had been going round in circles, trying to work out where he was. Looking at the paper, the young lady said, 'I know exactly where that is and I live close by, but I'm just on my way to a Christmas party. Would you like to come?' 'Sure,' was the enthusiastic reply. He could scarcely believe his luck.

At the next stop they left the train, hand in hand, laughing merrily. I said to myself as they disappeared into the crowd, 'Happy Christmas to you both.'

Julie had a close friend called Sylvia whom she had known since childhood. Sylvia was bridesmaid at Julie's wedding. Julie then went to live in another part of England and it was at this point Sylvia decided to see the world. Over the years the friends lost touch. Sylvia lived abroad for years and Julie moved to various parts of the country.

Twenty-five years later they both had two daughters of similar ages, and one of Julie's daughters, Michelle, became a journalist. On finishing her degree she obtained a reporter's job on a small Lancashire town's newspaper – the same Lancashire town Sylvia had eventually settled in, and nowhere near the area where the friends had grown up together. Sylvia gasped in astonishment at the sight of Michelle's picture in her local paper. She not only had the same very unusual surname as her friend, but looked remarkably like her mother at that age – the age Sylvia had last seen her. Jumping up, Sylvia went to the phone and rang the young reporter. To her delight she found that she was indeed her long lost friend's daughter.

An even stranger coincidence was that that very week Michelle and her father had decided to try and trace Sylvia, even writing an advertisement to put in a national newspaper. The young reporter had the copy in her handbag ready to place in the newspaper and was quite speechless to receive a phone call from the very person she was just about to try and find!

When I hear songs about home or hear someone speak about secure family backgrounds I think of Robert, who had never known any of these joys and securities. His young life had been one of turmoil and struggle. Along with his sister, he had spent most of his early years in a children's home. At the age of fifteen he had to leave the home, and he and his sister travelled to Israel to work on a kibbutz. In many ways, this was as difficult as the children's home. Few people spoke English and the mix of many different nationalities and a totally different way of life was a harrowing experience for the youngsters.

Robert could not settle. When he grew older he travelled all over Israel and beyond, a restless spirit.

Eventually both he and his sister married, Robert becoming a father to two boys and living again on a kibbutz. His sister, however, went to live in Africa with her new husband and they lost touch.

Ten years rolled by, until the summer of 1966, when two cousins of Robert's decided to visit Israel from their home in England. Robert's sister reported that there was still no news of him and that everyone had virtually given up hope. The cousins, Glenda and David, were starting to believe he did not want to be found. Israel is a fairly small country after all, and extensive research and inquiries had been made. They pressed on with their holiday, knowing there was little they could do to help.

The culmination of their trip was to be a visit to Jerusalem including the Wailing Wall. They discovered, however, they were not where they had planned to be. Previously, they had approached the square containing the Wall from a different quarter and were momentarily disoriented. They descended into the square down steep, narrow passageways, thronged with worshippers and tourists clamouring to get into the square. Of all the ways of approaching the square this was by far the most difficult and busiest.

At one point about half-way down the path there was a small square area at the end of one flight of steps. Positioned rather precariously on this small steep area was an army patrol hut. Outside on guard stood two soldiers trying to control the crowds. They had almost been swept past the soldiers when one suddenly turned to face them and to their astonishment said 'Hello'. The boy they had lost touch with so many years before was now a man and soldier in the army. He had recognized them. As they had been adults when he had last seen them, it was not too difficult. Momentarily taken aback, they soon realized it was Robert and with joy arranged to meet him when his duty finished, which was luckily in only thirty minutes' time.

The families are now all happily reunited but what were the chances of the cousins meeting like that, the timing, the area, the crowds? Was it 'mere' coincidence, or was it providence at work?

Sometimes an incident might appear to be insignificant and trivial, but to the person concerned it is vital. This is the story of a young girl about to take an exam. Finding one particular piece of information felt like the most important quest of her life, but its success came out of a lucky meeting. Her family had all tried very hard to help her and failed, so they contacted a neighbour, the Reverend Dennis Duckworth. Here is the story he told me:

My neighbour's daughter was about to take an exam and needed to know the precise words used by the Archbishop of Canterbury on presenting the Queen with a Bible at her Coronation. They had searched everywhere they could possibly think of to no avail, and then someone had suggested they contact myself. It was thought that as a minister of religion I might possibly have the answer. Alas, I did not, but I spent the entire following morning thumbing through reference books, encyclopaedias and every possible relevant source at my disposal. I too drew a blank.

At this point I felt as frustrated as the lady and her daughter; the exam was now only twenty-four hours away and they were no nearer the answer. I had let them down and the poor girl was getting quite distraught as only schoolgirls can.

My wife, having joined in the search and given up, said philosophically, 'We tried, but we obviously can do no more. You really must forget it.' That wasn't easy, but I had no other option. Late afternoon arrived and I was putting off the time when I must go to the neighbour and say I could not help. The exam was first thing the following morning so all seemed lost.

I heard the key in the door, my wife returning from a meeting. It had promised to be most interesting with a very knowledgeable speaker. I greeted her with the news that I was just about to go to the neighbour's and admit defeat, when she said, 'Believe it or not, at the end of the guest speaker's address she finished by saying, "I would now like to quote the words the Archbishop of Canterbury used when handing the

Queen a Bible at her Coronation", and proceeded to quote them.' My wife took them down for me. The day was saved – my credibility and the exam – wonderful synchronicity?

Sometimes a person may experience more than one coincidence in rapid succession, a cluster effect. They are much rarer than a single coincidence but often life-shaping, as Janine discovered. Looking back at the train of events and coincidences, she finds it hard to believe that there was not some grand plan in operation from a higher source than she could generate. It all began with an unexpected but fortunate meeting.

Articulate, bright and successful, Janine nevertheless found herself feeling nothing but despair. A long-established relationship that she had believed to be secure and happy suddenly ended in betrayal. They had met on a train years before in what she believed to be a happy coincidence. Now her partner revealed that he had met someone else and would be moving on. Career-wise, Janine had been increasingly unhappy for some time, wanting to move on but feeling trapped. Distressing physical problems of a close family member added to the heartache and despair she was feeling. Sitting down in her lovely home, which no longer gave her any pleasure, she tried to be positive and make plans. None emerged and melancholy hung around her like a fog. Sinking deeper into despair, there suddenly seemed only one way out of it all. Why go on? It was only for a moment, but in that deepening dark state ending her life seemed the only option. She sat motionless until the light faded, numb with cold and her own emotions.

Suddenly she realized, to compound her problems, that the following day she was scheduled to make an important presentation at work. Mercifully it was already prepared, but she had little heart for standing in front of colleagues and superiors and feigning enthusiasm. The thought did, however, serve to bring her back to reality and she went to bed pondering on the presentation instead of her own end.

The next day, as the hall slowly filled, Janine arranged her papers at the desk prior to beginning her speech. Outside, another meeting across the hall was coming to an end and people were gradually leaving. One man emerged from the room, glanced at his watch and realized he had just missed his train back to London. Silently cursing, he glanced through the glass doors opposite. Seeing Janine, he had the odd feeling they had met before. He read the announcement of the presentation and saw it was an area he was interested in and wished to extend in his own department in London. He now had time to kill so he wandered in and sat down, still puzzling where he had seen Janine before.

The presentation was a triumph. Janine had warmed to the subject for, relieved to have her mind lifted from personal problems, she threw herself into it and felt a rush of enthusiasm. The senior executive from London was most impressed and said so immediately after the meeting. They both realized at the same time that years before they had sat next to each other at a dinner-party and exclaimed at this coincidence. 'To think I almost missed your excellent presentation,' he said, 'and happy re-acquaintance.'

The following day, Janine received a phone call from London. It was the same senior executive offering her a job, to be accepted as swiftly as possible. Jumping at the chance, she could scarcely believe her good fortune but soon the practicalities of the situation hit home. What about her elderly sick relative so dependent upon her? How could she move 250 miles away and leave her? What of selling the house? Where would she live in London?

The following day in the office she told a fellow staff member of her dilemma. 'Well,' he said, 'I'm looking for a house in your area, the family needs more space. Perhaps I could come and look at it.' That evening he and his wife called, and loved it. The following day they made an offer. Janine accepted and within only days the house was sold. She then went to see her relative, wondering how on earth she would solve that problem. Arriving full of trepidation, she was amazed to find the elderly lady very perky and positive and bursting with news. 'I've decided to move into this local, beautiful rest-home. I feel I need help at hand round the clock these days,' she said. The rest-home was of the highest quality and places at a premium, but on making inquiries she had learned that a place had just become available so she decisively accepted on the spot.

Janine could scarcely believe it, the job of a lifetime handed to her, the house sold and her dependent relative cared for all in the space of a few days. The chain of events did not end there, however. Visiting her new department in London for the first time, she was informed of a local, helpful estate agent. There, simply waiting to be snapped up, with just a fifteen-minute walk to her new place of work, was the perfect flat.

As you might expect after so many coincidences, the move went smoothly. The job is challenging and exciting, new friends abound and life is happier than ever before. To add to all this, shortly after arriving in London, Janine met through colleagues a charming man with a twinkle in his eye and a zest for life that would complete her happy lifestyle.

There was a sequel to these fortunate events. One day, travelling north once more to visit friends some twelve months later, she was sitting on a train waiting for the time of departure when who should appear but the villain of the piece, the man who twelve months previously had left her feeling bereft and desperate. His new relationship had not worked out and he was astonished to hear of Janine's good fortune. He stood up to leave the train looking wistful and half suggesting they should renew their friendship. Janine smiled and said how fortunate and grateful she was that he had left. The train meeting had brought the story full circle and it really was time for him to get off.

The next story comes into the category of 'missed meetings', but is amusing and heart-warming in its outcome. I have a photograph album containing the most unspectacular view of Niagara Falls ever taken. True, my lack of prowess as a photographer is well-known amongst my family and friends, but this photograph is in the album not for the blurred image of the Falls but the large green Cadillac in the foreground.

The story began with a holiday in America. We had friends living not too far away from Niagara Falls, so it was arranged that we should meet at a central point to spend the weekend together at Niagara. It was also arranged, unknown to me at the time, that our friend's parents would join us if possible. Time-keeping was not their parents' strong suit and not turning up at all was also not unknown.

We met our friends and, sitting on the porch of a coffee shop, we chatted happily, catching up on the news whilst gazing mesmerized at the spectacular display Nature provided for us. It was at this point I took the photograph, trying hard to wait for a break in the traffic to obtain a clear view. The traffic was incessant, but eventually, in a short lull, I quickly snapped the scene.

An hour or so passed and we were getting restless. My friend concluded that her parents were not going to turn up and we might as well move along. On the Sunday morning, my friend rang her parents and rather crossly asked why they had failed to turn up. 'We did,' they protested, but were not really believed. Impatiently, my friend put the phone down. 'Typical,' she muttered.

Putting our cases in the car for the trip to the airport we went for one last stroll around and a visit to the 'overnight film developer' to collect our snaps. They were not terrific by any standard, so I was taken aback when my friend gasped at the shot I had taken from the coffee shop. She suddenly started to laugh, for the large green Cadillac driving past in the foreground of the picture was her parents' car, and there wearing a puzzled expression was her father behind the wheel. They had after all driven all the way from upstate New York only to have missed us by minutes!

LUCKY ESCAPES

The quotation at the beginning of this book is by Emanuel Swedenborg and refers to choices and free will. Do we choose to believe that our lives have a pattern and is that pattern laid out by divine providence? The experiences described in this book suggest that there are signposts in our daily lives in the form of guidance, symbolism and synchronistic events. At the same time, we can make use of our will and wisdom when making choices. The truth, as the saying goes, is out there, but we have to advance towards it, and if we are too dismissive of, or choose to ignore, the signposts, we may miss it altogether. Sometimes, of course, the freedom to choose can lead us into danger. We may even hear an inner warning voice, but deliberately ignore it and there are elements of this in our next story.

Rosie knew almost immediately that she had made a terrible mistake. She had been at a party until the early hours of the morning, and then decided to walk home. It was an area of Liverpool she knew well, it was not far to her flat, and the roads were well lit. Yet at 1.30 a.m. as she found herself walking home alone, she became more frightened with every step. All the horror stories about women alone flooded through her head as she realized she had come too far to turn back and would have to keep walking. The road was quiet, strangely bereft of traffic and even the houses looked dark and unfriendly, not a light at any window.

Suddenly, she heard footsteps behind her. Turning to look and shaking with fright, she was relieved to see it was another woman, hurrying to catch up with her. Breathless, the woman reached her. She too had made a similar silly decision, having elected to walk home but instantly regretted it. Feeling confident in each other's company, they walked together, relieved to hear they lived very close to each other, on opposite corners. There was an instant rapport as they chatted with ease, discovering they had similar jobs and pastimes, and before they knew it they were home. Rosie said, 'We must keep in touch. Call tomorrow and we'll have coffee,' feeling sure she had found a new friend. The other woman smiled and readily agreed. 'By the way,' she said, 'my name is Rosie Ballantyne.' Rosie's mouth fell open. It is not a common name, but her surname was also Ballantyne!

Many stories of coincidence feature narrowly escaping a possibly fatal accident. So many of these stories reached me I had to omit many for fear of repetition. Cars feature strongly in several accounts, which leave one wondering whether these escapes are the result of premonitions, angelic intervention or real miracles of modern times.

Amanda believes her escape was miraculous. One summer day, she was invited to the birthday celebration of a close friend. Having a reputation as an excellent baker of cakes, it was a foregone conclusion that she would provide the celebratory cake.

The confection was a piece of art. Piled high with strawberries and cream, it was a delight to the eye. In mid-afternoon Amanda prepared to leave for this 'women only' tea party. Wearing a light summer dress, she set forth, car keys in one hand, cake in the other. She decided to deposit the cake on the rear seat of the car and drive slowly, keeping an eye on it.

Her house was situated close to a long sweeping bend in the road in a quiet village with very little traffic in the middle of the afternoon. Balancing the cake in her left hand she struggled a little opening the car door. To this day she is unsure as to what exactly happened next, but to her dismay she dropped the precious cake. Covered only with loose cling film it splattered all over her dress, the car and the middle of the road. Cursing, Amanda stomped into the house to clean herself and then find a dustpan and brush to clear the road with. No sooner had she reached her front door than there was a loud crunching sound. Spinning round, she saw a car had taken the bend too quickly, lost control and smashed directly into her car, which was virtually demolished – at the very point where seconds earlier she had dropped the cake. But for losing her grip on the cake, the car would have smashed into her too.

The driver of the car was stunned and shaken but unhurt. It was clear, however, that Amanda would not have survived.

My second car story occurred in Australia in the summer of 1996. Susan was taking her three children to visit their grandfather. Susan's mother was accompanying them on this visit also and as Susan and her mother chatted, they became aware of the children squabbling in the back of the car. Susan asked them to be quiet as their arguments were distracting her and breaking her concentration on the road.

Eventually, there was nothing for it but to stop and forcibly reprimand the children for their behaviour. Peace reigned, everyone settled down and Susan started the car once more. The road was narrow and contained some dangerous corners. Susan approached the first corner and was taken aback by the speed of a car hurtling towards her on the wrong side of the road. The car was 'fish-tailing', screeching round corners, and the driver appeared to have momentarily lost control.

Fortunately, Susan was driving cautiously and had time to slow right down as the car went speeding past, narrowly missing them. Collecting her thoughts, she stopped again for a moment before driving off, only to be confronted by a second car, also speeding and on the wrong side of the road. It seemed they had been spared twice in only a few minutes. She thought instantly of how different the outcome would have been had she not stopped the car briefly to talk to the children, for she would surely have been further along the road and have met one of these vehicles head on. Having a strong religious faith, Susan firmly believes that day they were saved by some form of divine intervention.

Our third story concerning cars comes from a woman in the Czech Republic. Alice lives in a small town named Vysoké Mýtó, where she is a teacher. One day, driving along by herself in the car, she suddenly worried about some sheet music she was supposed to be taking with her. Eventually, she pulled over and stopped the car to search her briefcase and put her mind at rest. Looking through her case, she found the music, much to her relief.

Glancing up at this point, she noticed a car pass her stationary vehicle. Fastening her case, she set off again, shortly arriving at a sharp curve in the road. There she saw the car that had passed her only minutes before, now a total wreck having crashed into an oncoming car, which she could only assume had been in the middle of the road. Thankfully, no one was seriously hurt even though the cars were extremely badly damaged.

Alice realized her anxiety regarding the sheet music had prevented her from being involved with the oncoming car and she silently gave thanks that she had stopped in time. Alice was a new and inexperienced driver and she felt sure the accident would have had a more serious outcome. Premonition or guidance yet again?

THE NATURAL WORLD

There is a basic pattern which underlies all the stories in this book, and that is order coming out of apparent chaos. We may sometimes feel our lives are chaotic, but over the last couple of decades scientists have started to introduce another meaning to chaos, which is both positive and creative. Chaos theory has come about because scientists have started to realize that in all sorts of things in which they had been unable to see patterns there is some very subtle, complex and even sophisticated organization. Most of the best examples of this are taken from the natural world, including ferns, snowflakes, DNA, and the human circulatory system.

I should now like to look at some stories in which the natural world features strongly. They are perhaps not all coincidence stories exactly, but they show us patterns in Nature, organization, and maybe even a form of intelligence which we can't really explain. For example, the monarch butterfly is one of nature's most remarkable wonders. Every year this tiny, fragile insect flies 3000 miles from the city of Toronto in Canada to the forest glades in Mexico and back again in an annual mating cycle.

A story involving the monarch butterfly relates appropriately to a magazine called *Chrysalis*. The publishers were contemplating metamorphosis, amalgamating several editions of the magazine into book form. Some time earlier, the editor had been given a milkweed branch containing a large green-and-black caterpillar. The day the proposal was made, the now black chrysalis on the branch became transparent, displaying the orange-and-black folded pattern within. Later that day, when the decision was made to turn *Chrysalis* into a series of books, a monarch butterfly emerged.

Many miracles of Nature seem to happen independently of human beings, but some stories, including the next two, show a connection between human beings and the natural world.

Joni Mitchell, the gifted Canadian singer, was making an album with the legendary jazz musician, Charlie Mingus. So revered is Charlie in jazz circles that he has been referred to as a musical mystic. The album was being recorded in Mexico and everything was progressing splendidly. The two artists were working well together and enjoying the experience.

The shock was tremendous when, half-way through recording, Charlie Mingus died. It was 5 January 1979 and he was mourned throughout the jazz world. Joni Mitchell was deeply moved and went on to complete the album alone and dedicate it to Charlie by calling it *Mingus*.

Cremation took place the day after Charlie died amid tributes and great homage to an irreplaceable artist. On the same day a most extraordinary incident occurred: fifty-six whales beached themselves on the Mexican coastline where they died swiftly. Charlie Mingus was fifty-six years old. These events led Joni Mitchell to say: 'These are the coincidences that thrill my imagination.'

Children often have a great affinity with Nature and the earth. I recall vividly my daughter, when small, planting a bluebell bulb. She dug the bulb up on a regular basis to see if it was growing. Miraculously, it did and the garden now has a large bluebell patch.

The Findhorn Foundation in Scotland has become known, amongst many other things, for the enormous vegetables grown in its grounds. This may be seen as a miracle, for initially the ground was infertile, yet the community produced vegetables of size and quantity unknown before in any part of Scotland. It was as if Nature was responding to the love and care invested in the project. Some time ago a guest on an Oprah Winfrey show produced evidence that if plants were prayed for they would grow stronger and faster than the control plants.

Eva was a little girl whose affinity with Nature, love for an aunt and belief in God produced a modern-day miracle. She believes the power of prayer helped.

Eva grew up in the former Yugoslavia, a happy child for the most part in a loving family and a then peaceful country. She had an aunt of whom she was especially fond. They had such a rapport that Eva felt she could share almost anything with her and she would understand. Her aunt had no children of her own, whereas Eva's mother had four, and so the aunt had more time to listen to the little girl. Sadly, when Eva was seven years old her beloved aunt died. The whole family missed her terribly, but Eva was inconsolable. Her father, in an attempt to take her mind off the tragedy and involve her in his life more, taught her to garden. They had a vegetable plot and grew fruits also, to help the family food requirements.

Summer came and it was decided to take a short holiday. They all felt they needed a break and Eva was beginning to feel better and quite cheerful. The idea of the holiday excited her, but as the time to leave approached she began to wish her aunt could have accompanied them. It was an area they knew the aunt had visited and loved.

Eva's father suggested that Eva should place a plant in the earth at the holiday site to grow in her aunt's memory and give pleasure to others. Eva thought this a marvellous plan, but instead of a flowering shrub she wanted to grow strawberries. Arguing correctly that her aunt had loved strawberries, the most fitting gift would be a strawberry plant.

This was agreed, but there was one problem. Eva's father was unhappy with the condition of the soil for planting. It was completely wrong, he insisted, but, undaunted, the little girl put the plant in the ground by the edge of the wood. Several days later, as they were due to leave, it was already looking decidedly sickly. Eva sat alone next to it, willing it to grow. At this point she remembered words her teacher had given her and her class not too long ago. 'Problems are better shared, share yours with God.' Eva closed her eyes and told God how much she wished the strawberry plant to grow. She urged Him to see how special it was and how much she had loved her aunt. As a result she felt much better, and watered it for the last time before setting out for home.

Years passed, and Eva grew up. One day, by coincidence, she met a young man who had grown up in the little village where they had stayed so long ago. Eva told him the story about her aunt and her strawberry plant. He listened in silence and then said, 'We will visit my village. I will take you to see the place so special to you.'

Driving along in the car, Eva imagined her nice young man was smiling to himself. 'Perhaps he has a secret,' she thought. Eventually, they arrived at the village, now slightly larger but still unspoilt. They parked the car and walked up the slope towards the woods. Turning the corner at the top of the incline and on the edge of the wood, Eva caught her breath. The young man's secret smile widened into a broad grin, for there, as far as the eye could see, was a carpet of wild strawberries!

TELEPATHIC COMMUNICATION

I have already mentioned Carl Jung's theory of the collective unconscious, which contains a pool of images and memories through which we are all connected. Some stories of synchronicity, especially examples of people bumping into each other in unexpected places, make one wonder if we could be connected in unsuspected ways. Are we in fact giving off signals or 'vibes' which influence the behaviour of others? Could even alter their movements resulting in them unconsciously walking towards us instead of in another direction? It is not beyond the realms of possibility.

Telepathy is a well-documented mind activity, and we may be exercising this ability without even realizing it.

Impressive though such unexpected encounters and reunions are, even more inexplicable are the examples of synchronicity linked by thousands of miles. The following accounts give some very recent and remarkable examples. The first incident was related to me by an American woman living in England. She felt very unwell one evening with an excruciating headache. Since she was not a migraine sufferer and not under any stress at all, the cause was a mystery. She thought it likely that she was experiencing early symptoms of an illness and went to bed early to rest. Morning arrived and she felt fine, not even a slight headache, so she went to work as usual.

Later that day, she received a phone call from America informing her that her sister was in hospital. She had fallen from her horse and received head injuries but was expected to recover fully. When the time difference was taken into consideration, the woman realized that the fall had occurred simultaneously with her severe headache.

Two stories concerning events linking England and Australia follow, one happy and one very sad. The latter concerns an Australian woman living in England. She had not been away from home long and one day began to feel very restless. It was not easy to identify this feeling. It did not feel exactly like the pangs of homesickness she felt occasionally, but was a definite unease. All day she was unable to concentrate or accomplish anything at all and that night sleep would not come and relieve her of this odd restlessness. The following day, however, she received a phone call from Australia to say that her closest friend had been in a horrific road accident and was seriously ill.

The third example of long-distance synchronicity is much happier. It involves a man whose brother and sis-ter-in-law lived in Australia. This man was renowned as a deep sleeper, never having trouble getting to sleep and never ever, as far as he could remember, waking until morning. This being the case, he was astonished one night to find himself wide awake at 3 a.m. He sat up in bed mystified, as there had been no noise or any other reason to wake up, so after gazing through the window to ensure all was quiet, he promptly went back to sleep.

The mystery was solved when his brother rang the following day to announce that their baby had been born. 'I didn't ring you at the time of the birth', he said, 'because it would have been 3 a.m. and I didn't want to wake you.' 'Nevertheless you did!' came the laughing response.

* * * 2 * * *

Spiritual Coincidences

'The angels went on to say that all things, in fact the smallest of all things, and even the smallest of the smallest, are directed by the Lord's Providence, down to the very steps taken by the feet.'

EMANUEL SWEDENBORG

Coincidences such as the ones described in the last chapter can be astonishing, comforting, bewildering, highly amusing or a source of joy for those involved. There are also many examples of how such events relate to religious or spiritual belief. These could be called spiritual coincidences, and I should like to explore this theme in this chapter.

Numerous spiritual traditions have a strong belief in the involvement of God (however pictured or understood) in our earthly life. The above quotation is one example from the Christian tradition. It is interesting to see what happens if we start to interpret such events as spiritual experience. People who have had a supernatural experience are not in the majority. Although there are many programmes on television today about such phenomena as near-death experiences, visions, and angelic visitations, those with authentic stories to tell are few and far between. We may, however, only be aware of the tip of the iceberg, since only a minority of people are prepared to relate their experiences.

Coincidences, on the other hand, are universal experiences. They are often major life-changing experiences or link with what people regard as the fundamentals of their life. They may therefore be a type of universal spiritual experience which is open to all.

Those who see coincidences as meaningful are likely to be people who have some sort of spiritual belief. Although many of those with whom I have talked on this subject express this in formal religious terms, there are others for whom it takes a more fluid form of harmony, pattern and purpose in life. This chapter looks at examples of events which those involved interpret as demonstrating a spiritual order at work.

PRIESTLY COINCIDENCES

Here is a story from a theological student. Such experiences are by no means reserved to those involved in priestly work although, having taken the big decision to embark on such a change of direction, they may be more inclined to reflect in this way about their lives.

This impressive and rather 'shiver provoking' story concerns a mature student called Alan. In his middle years, Alan decided he wanted to be a minister of religion. As a theological student, he had a book allowance, but as every student knows there are always many more books they find attractive than the allowance will provide for. One book Alan bought and enjoyed was *Mister God, This Is Anna* and, wanting to share this with his wife, he gave it to her on one of her many visits to the North. She loved the book and wanted to keep it, intending to 'dip into it' from time to time.

Weeks passed and Alan realized he missed the book and thought perhaps he should buy another copy. One Saturday he visited a local open-air market full of food stalls, families and second-hand book stalls. After a good browse, Alan noticed a copy of *Mister God, This Is Anna* on a shelf at the back of the stall priced at a mere £1. For reasons he himself never quite understood he deliberated and eventually walked away without buying it.

No sooner had he returned to college than he regretted his decision and said to a colleague, 'I can't believe I left it on the shelf – it almost had my name on it.' The incident was soon forgotten and weeks passed before Alan had the opportunity to visit the market again. There was the book, still on the shelf at the back of the stall. This time he didn't hesitate but swiftly bought the book. On returning to college, he lifted it out of his shopping carrier and showed his colleague the book. As he opened it he gasped in astonishment, for there on the fly leaf, written in an unknown hand, was his name.

Julian is a minister of religion in Sydney, Australia, but his spiritual coincidence happened when he lived and worked as a minister in Birmingham, England. He was involved in a retreat, held in Warwickshire, which was to last for a week and included some very interesting speakers. One speaker was the eminent Cambridge linguist Dr John Chadwick, whose session involved an in-depth study of the Lord's Prayer. Julian found the presentation thought-provoking and deeply moving. On arriving home to his church in Birmingham, Julian knew he would give the prayer more attention and study, having learned so much of its history.

Walking into his study, he noticed a rolled-up poster with a handwritten message from one of his young church members. The young man had been to a printing and publication exhibition at the National Exhibition Centre in Birmingham. He explained that he had seen the poster and immediately thought of Julian. He had left it with best wishes as a nice surprise on his return. Intrigued, Julian unrolled the poster. It was a large, beautifully illuminated, calligraphic version of the Lord's Prayer.

SPIRITUAL TELEPATHY

The previous two stories centre on tangible objects, but what about the spiritual synchronicity of minds? Everyone has had the experience of thinking about someone and then bumping into them in the street. Or you walk to the telephone to ring someone but before you arrive it rings and the very person you were about to contact is on the phone. However, if we compare this with other more complex instances involving more than a simple one-to-one link, we have to start wondering if there is some 'higher' level of spiritual input. It has been well documented that certain numbers and dates play an important part in people's lives and indeed deaths. Many people die on their birthdays, Ingrid Bergman for instance. People have been known to predict the day of their death even when in good health. Does this suggest an ability to choose when to die? This ability and a subconscious spiritual telepathy appears to be involved in our next story. The spiritual contact and connections in this story leave us in little doubt that there was a powerful spiritual synchronicity at work.

Julie looked after her elderly aunt and uncle. They

had no children of their own and thus their niece was close to them. In time they both became hospitalized, with different but serious illnesses. Having been so close all their lives they found the separation at this time difficult to bear. Their respective wards, although belonging to the same hospital, were in different buildings. Their niece found visiting difficult with the problem facing her of often visiting the hospital twice in one day and either spending each whole visiting period with one of them or splitting one visiting time in half and dashing from one side of the hospital site to another. Failing rapidly, not least because they were separated, their spirits sank as low as their physical state and it became difficult to know how to cheer them.

One visiting day Julie arrived to find her uncle fading fast. She sat holding his hand, and in minutes he had passed away. Sadly, she stood to leave, knowing she then had to go and break the news to his wife. Crossing the hospital grounds, she entered the women's section wondering how exactly to tell her aunt. She arrived at her ward, having completed the ten minutes it took her to walk across, to be met by a nurse with the news that her aunt had died ten minutes earlier — at the exact moment that Julie's uncle had died.

It is difficult not to feel in such a case that death is not a cutting-off and ending of life but a transcendence of the limitations of life in this world. There are also many stories of people who feel that relatives die on a date which was somehow already significant to those concerned.

Dates and public events sometimes combine in bizarre ways, as in the case of two assassinated US presidents. President John Kennedy was elected exactly 100 years after Abraham Lincoln. Both were assassinated on a Friday in the presence of their wives. Each lost a son whilst living in the White House. Lincoln was killed in Ford's Theatre, Kennedy in a Ford-made Lincoln convertible. Kennedy's assassin fled from a warehouse into a theatre, Lincoln's from a theatre to a warehouse. Lincoln's killer was born in 1839, Kennedy's in 1939. Both presidents were succeeded by men called Johnson. Lincoln's secretary was called Kennedy and begged him not to go to the theatre. Kennedy's secretary was named Lincoln and strongly advised him not to go to Dallas.

It is clear therefore that not all such coincidences are of a joyous nature, and important events may be linked to great sorrow.

Barbara and Peter, for instance, who found they had to cope with the loss of a son, looked back and saw a date pattern which surprised them. Their son, Robert, was diagnosed as having cancer and inevitably many hospital appointments ensued. He received conventional hospital treatment but also help from a healer who became a firm family friend. He was treated at

Great Ormond Street Children's Hospital in London for quite some time, initially with much success. With another son and daughter to look after as well it was obviously a busy and worrying time for Barbara and Peter.

After Robert died in hospital early one morning, his sister told Barbara she heard him call her name. Looking at Robert's appointment card after his death, Barbara realized for the first time how significant the dates had been. Firstly, he had been to see the consultant on his mother's birthday, then on his own birthday, his sister's, his parents' wedding anniversary and again on his mother's birthday. The visits were several weeks apart and so it does seem very significant.

THE POWER OF PRAYER AND FAITH

During our lives we may experience situations which do not involve the death of a person yet symbolize death and new life. Many people seeking guidance from Tarot cards are relieved to find that a card representing death can mean that one aspect or area of one's life is about to vanish and a new venture begin. Every year, the miracle of spring underlines this for us. On a cold winter's day, with trees forming bleak silhouettes against a grey sky, it is hard to believe they will be green and full of life again in a few months. Yet every year brings a rebirth in springtime.

New beginnings in our lives can be very dramatic and we know the changes will ensure our lives will literally never be the same again. This was the case for Janice who, with her husband Mark, decided after lengthy deliberations to embark on a new life in America. Once there, difficulties arose. They needed to find an apartment, employment, and many practical essential items like a car had to be purchased.

Mark had been very involved in teaching Reiki and yoga and he had hoped the opportunity to practise in Chicago would present itself. Despite inquiries, scouring magazines and so on, there did not appear to be any such groups or openings in the area. Janice worried about this and one day her worry and homesickness became overwhelming. Had they made the right decision? Where to go from here? Janice, however, believed in angels and silently she asked her angel to help, to give her a sign that all would be well.

The following day, Mark went to a local shop to use a photocopying machine. A woman was photocopying pages from a book, so he stood patiently waiting his turn. When she finished her photocopying and lifted the book from the machine, he saw that the book was about Reiki. Scarcely believing his eyes, he engaged the lady in conversation and learned she belonged to a group to which he and Janice were cordially invited.

There was a centre with rooms available for the practice of Reiki and yoga. The angel had truly given them the requested sign.

René told me that the first coincidence he experienced had changed his life and his attitudes. He had hit a very bad patch in life, struggling to find employment although talented and qualified. He moved flats many times to help juggle finances and was at a low ebb. Talking with a friend one evening, he confessed to feeling thoroughly miserable and unable to see any way out of his predicament.

The friend said in a very matter-of-fact way, 'You're a Christian — why don't you pray for a job?' René looked at him in astonishment. It was true that he was a Christian, but he had only ever prayed for spiritual help. It had never occurred to him to ask God for everyday, practical help. After his friend left, he sat for a long time thinking about what he had said. Surely God would not reproach him for asking for practical help and maybe praying would make him feel better.

He began to pray, telling God how he felt and how desperately he needed a job. Afterwards he felt better and had a strong feeling that he should leave things to divine providence. Even so he was stunned when only two weeks later he was offered a job. This happened eight years ago and René has applied and secured a more advanced position since then and never encountered the problem of unemployment again. A mere coincidence, or a divine intervention with the powerful message – trust?

Sometimes a simple solution to a problem can be so obvious no-one had considered it. This was the case for Judith: a dramatic incident helped her find the answer to a very everyday problem.

Working as a supply teacher, Judith arrived one day at a Roman Catholic day school, willing to help wherever she was most needed. The headteacher assigned her to a one-to-one session with a small boy for whom reading was becoming a severe problem. It was decided that a teacher's undivided attention might help a great deal.

The session was going badly and Judith did not seem to be able to reach him, but she was dismayed at the reading material she was supposed to inspire him with. In all her years of teaching she had never encountered anything so dull. What should she do? As a conscientious teacher she felt quite depressed at the way the lesson was evolving. Walking slowly around the small room she suddenly glanced up and saw a simple crucifix on the wall. The second her eyes alighted on this she felt a powerful surge of energy striking her so violently it was almost like an electric shock. Scarcely able to breathe, she was astonished to hear a voice say, 'Let him choose.' What a simple, normal instruction, she thought.

Collecting herself and calming down, she took the little boy's hand and together they went to the school library. 'Choose anything you wish,' she said and waited patiently while the little boy explored. Some time later he appeared, eyes shining, with several books about dinosaurs tucked under his arm. It had not occurred to anyone to find out what interested the little boy and he had simply been chained to a boring reading project. Arriving back in the classroom the boy eagerly opened his books and there followed a most rewarding session, which Judith remembers with joy to this day.

The breakthrough had been made, he was on his way. Judith stared at the cross. What power had emanated from that simple wooden symbol! She was not a Roman Catholic, not even of the Christian faith, but she had received spiritual guidance that day without a doubt.

Mary's story contains a series of linked coincidences, which she found life-affirming and inspirational. I shall let Mary tell you her story which begins in the summer of 1996.

'When I was asked by the minister who was to preach at my induction as an assistant minister into my first pastorate if there was a particular theme that I would find helpful, I was not aware of making a momentous decision, or one that would have repercussions beyond the service itself. He mentioned several themes that had come into his mind. Immediately "the pot in the hands of the Potter" felt good. I did not respond at the time, since he asked me to think about it and let him know. He very much wanted the sermon to be helpful for me and saw the induction as a partnership between congregation and minister.

'When he rang again I was able to say that the theme of the Potter in Jeremiah, Chapter 18 felt good. I warmed to the idea of being reshaped for the people I would minister to. I felt a need to be in a different mould, no longer a student but a minister. Together with my congregation, we would need to allow the Lord to reshape us so that we could work together doing His will, not our own.

'Less than a fortnight after my induction I began following a course of spiritual exercises, using the approach of St Ignatius. This was to be the basis of my daily devotions, the source and inspiration for my daily work. The first week's theme was "Listen, I stand at the door and knock" (Revelation 3:20). The day I began the exercises I was at a residential ministers' seminar. I had been meditating on these words in the morning. I felt them affirmed in my life when I heard them spoken at the holy communion service later that day. They formed the theme of the service.

'The following day I again felt surrounded by heaven when I glanced at the prayer suggestion for the second week, "Be the Potter", based on Jeremiah, Chapter 18. As the first female minister in our church organization, it felt like an affirmation that I was in the right place, that heaven was with me, supporting me, there in its power and strength.

'Such affirmation has continued. For example, I had been given a book token to mark my inauguration into the assistant ministry of the church. It felt right to buy a Bible with it to allow me to take the Word of God to people where they are and share it with them. I found just what I wanted, a lovely maroon soft leather-backed, small New King James Version. When I got it home and opened it where the ribbon marker lay, I stood and stared as I read once again:

I went down to the Potter's house, and there he was, making something at the wheel. And the vessel that he made of clay was marred in the hands of the Potter; so he made it again into another vessel, as it seemed good to the Potter to make.

Then the word of the Lord came to me saying:

"O House of Israel, can I not do with you as this Potter?" says the Lord. "Look, as the clay is in the Potter's hand, so are you in my hand, O House of Israel!"

Jeremiah 18:4-6 NKJV

MIRACULOUS ESCAPES

Most people familiar with the City Centre of Manchester would agree that the most popular spot is St Anne's Square. Elegant and dignified, it retains all its original buildings, including a glass-domed arcade and the magnificent Royal Exchange, once the busy commercial centre for the satellite cotton towns surrounding the City. The gem of this lovely Square is the church from which it takes its name, St Anne's, the very heart of the old Centre. Like many of the country's churches, however, early in 1996 it was badly in need of renovation and repair. The cost was enormous but the work had to be done and the task was undertaken.

Central to these alterations was the organ. So specialized was the job of renovation that it was removed from the church to be repaired by experts. Early summer arrived and the church was looking splendid, but the organ was still not ready. All else was finished but the organ was several weeks overdue, though expected in a few more days.

June was blazing hot and the Saturday of 15 June dawned, ready to receive thousands of shoppers to the City Centre. The newly-renovated church was also ready for a busy day of visitors. Then the unthinkable happened. A huge bomb ripped the heart out of Manchester and shoppers fled screaming to avoid falling masonry and flying glass. The Royal Exchange was damaged and would be unusable for years to come. The elegant Square was covered in glass and debris as the shop windows shattered. St Anne's, newly fresh and clean, also caught the blast. The stained-glass windows were shattered and all the restoration work was undone.

Amongst all this devastation however, one bright note, or modern-day miracle, depending on one's point of view, was that the organ had not been replaced on the date planned. All the work and huge expense would have been in vain. St Anne's and its organist, Mr Ronald Frost, must have breathed a huge sigh of relief.

Another explosion which affected a church occurred at the West Side Baptist Church in Beatrice, Nebraska, on 1 March 1950. Exactly three minutes before a choir practice was due to start (7.27 p.m.) a gas explosion blew the church apart. The blast came from the basement right under the choir loft. Every member of the usually punctual, well-attended choir was late. Normally most of the choir would arrive early.

For twenty minutes after the blast the full implication of the coincidences unfolded like a miracle. People had been detained due to trivial everyday occurrences – finishing ironing, completing some piece of homework, a watch losing time, or being absorbed in a radio programme. The choir slowly arrived to see the devastation caused by the blast. They had all heard it of course, but never suspected their church was involved. They eventually realized that every single choir member was safe. All are convinced a divine hand engineered their salvation that night.

DIVINE MESSAGES

Do you believe divine messages appear in the most ordinary everyday items? Sometimes it is difficult not to. It was in March 1990 in Leicester that Faridan Kassam sliced open an aubergine and saw the seeds were spelling the name of God in Arabic script 'Ya-Allah'. It became an overnight sensation and was hailed as a modern miracle.

Laura's story has, I feel, similar connotations but this time the message came through a video tape. I shall allow Laura to tell her story.

'My favourite film, from the very first time I saw it, is *The Mission*. It touches me deeply and I never cease to be moved by it. Early in 1996 the film was shown on television and I decided to record it. I programmed the VCR and later put the video in its box for future viewing, but there was never enough time to watch it. Life was not without its problems at this time. My job was a particular source of worry, insecure and far from enjoyable, and a pervading sense of insecurity hung in the air for many reasons.

'One night, fairly late, I was ironing. My husband was not yet home from choir practice and I was not ready for sleep, so I decided to continue with the rather large pile of ironing and watch my video of *The Mission* at last.

'The film worked its usual magic and I was soon deeply enthralled in the historical drama. Suddenly, without warning, the film changed from colour to black and white and a young man in modern dress said, "The old life has to go, now is the time for change". At this point the film once more resumed and I was back in *The Mission*, in colour, at the point at which it had been interrupted.

'Shaken and bemused, I tried to work out what had happened. I had recorded the film on a BBC channel so it wasn't a commercial break. The video had not stopped at any point, so what could the explanation be? The message was clear enough, however, and I decided it was an omen meant for me. I took decisive action and new doors have opened. New optimism fills me and even dreams since that time have linking themes. It's still very puzzling but like a puzzle the pieces are slowly falling into place.'

Most people have a favourite song, or a piece of music that is very meaningful. For Helen this piece of special music was the song 'Morning Has Broken'. Her earliest memory of her mother was the sight of her pottering around the house singing this song. When I asked if her mother sang beautifully, Helen laughed. 'Not at all,' she said. 'My mother had the worst voice in the world and rarely managed to hit more than the odd note or two correctly.' Her mother's odd, tuneless rendition of the song frequently sprang to mind, evoking memories of warmth, comfort, security and love.

In her early teens Helen recalls Cat Stevens making a recording of the song which she played frequently over the years. When Helen was only in her early twenties her mother died and it was an obvious choice to sing 'Morning Has Broken' at her funeral. The song became the very epitome of everything Helen held dear.

Several years passed and Helen began to feel restless and discontented with her life and work. Out of the blue, she chanced upon an advertisement for a job in Toronto, Canada, which she successfully applied for.

The first week in Toronto was a blur, with so much to absorb. The new job looked interesting, the city large and attractive, and the suburb where initially she had been found a small apartment seemed pleasant enough. On Sunday Helen decided to go for a walk to get her local bearings. As she walked down a long, unfamiliar avenue, a wave of homesickness swept over her. Everything and everyone loved and familiar were thousands of miles away. How would she cope? At this point she realized she had reached the gate of a very pretty little church. The car park was full and a late-comer was hurrying inside. On impulse, Helen decided to go in, not even noticing the church's denomination.

As quietly as possible, Helen pushed open the main door. It was large and heavy but swung open with ease. She stepped inside to see the congregation rise to sing the first hymn and they sang out with full voice 'Morning Has Broken'. Helen immediately knew this was a sign and her own private mini-miracle telling her to have faith, that all would be well, and indeed it was.

*** 3 ***

The 'Arts' File

'To see a World in a Grain of Sand,
And a Heaven in a Wild Flower,
Hold Infinity in the palm of your hand,
And Eternity in an hour'

WILLIAM BLAKE

I have a theory that artists of all persuasions are more likely to experience synchronicity in their lives than other members of society. By their very nature they are more sensitive and open to the unknown and mysterious.

A high proportion of writers, actors, painters and musicians have had many coincidences in their lives. There are two famous examples of this in Ken Anderson's book, *Coincidence*. The first involves the film-star Julie Christie. In the film, *Don't Look Now*, Julie Christie and her screen husband (Donald Sutherland) are haunted by the spirit of their child who has drowned in a duck pond in their country house. Years later, Christie was visiting her farmhouse in Wales, looked after for her by a married couple, when she came upon the body of the couple's twenty-two-month-old son floating in the duck pond. She waded in to recover the body, mirroring the film scene.

Another remarkable true story concerns the actor Anthony Hopkins. In 1971, George Feifer's personal copy of his novel, *The Girl from Petrovka*, heavily annotated in the margins, had been stolen from Mr Feifer's car while it was parked in a London street. Two years later, the film rights of the novel were sold and Anthony Hopkins, who was to be the film's star, tried to buy a copy of the book but, despite trying several bookshops, he could not find a copy in stock. Disappointed, he started his journey back home. On his way, he noticed an open parcel on a seat in London's Leicester Square Underground station. He half suspected this to be a bomb and inspected it with caution, but to his relief it was a book. Delighted, he discovered it was a copy of the novel he had set out to buy. Later, in Vienna, the film star showed it to Mr Feifer when they met. Incredibly, it was the author's own personal copy stolen two years previously.

The next amazing story was related to me by Paul McNeilly, an actor and playwright. Paul had been writing his play for months. For the most part it had flowed, and he felt satisfied. His previous creations had been successful both in London and at the Edinburgh Festival, so he was well aware of what he was aiming for and what he believed would interest his audience. Gradually it all fell into place, except for one irritating aspect. The conclusion was eluding him, and he needed one important idea to tie the whole play together with impact. Several times he wrote endings for the play, but each time they did not work. He knew that none was the ending he was searching for and he grew impatient for inspiration.

After a frustrating morning, Paul realized that what he needed was a break and some exercise. Pulling on a coat and scarf, he set off. It felt good to be moving, and he quickened his pace and after some time, having paid little attention to his surroundings, he became aware of just how far he had walked. He realized with surprise he was in the vicinity of an old friend whom he was not in the habit of visiting at his home and whom he had not seen for some time. Finding himself almost on his doorstep, it seemed a good idea to call and say hello.

To Paul's delight, his friend was home and pleased to see him, if also a little surprised. He was warmly invited in and introduced to a third man who was drinking coffee and eager to chat. The conversation prior to Paul's arrival had been about books, the kind of conversation Paul enjoyed, so he joined in enthusiastically. The third man was strangely familiar and grew increasingly so as the conversation evolved. Suddenly, the man picked up the book he had brought and to illustrate a point said, 'Listen to this.' Paul was transfixed, but suddenly realized why the man seemed so familiar. It dawned on him at that moment that the man was the image of his play's main character. In addition, the passage he read from the book was exactly the idea he needed. Paul was immediately inspired to complete the play whose ending had proved so elusive. *Guinevere's Children*, will be performed at the Edinburgh Festival of 1997 and probably thereafter in London.

Books provide plenty of opportunities for synchronicity. Perhaps it is a case of coming across a book just when it is needed, or finding on one's shelves a forgotten tome which at that moment takes on a special resonance. Browsers in second-hand bookshops are full of tales of how exactly the right book for a particular interest or project has come into their possession. I have even heard of books apparently taking matters into their own hands by leaping off the shelves. Raymond Moody described this happening to him with a book which led him along the path to writing *Reunions*. People often find ideas in a book they are reading reappearing in discussions with friends, on radio or television or in newspaper articles at the same time. Here are some examples of life-changing coincidences featuring books.

Birthdays are special, no matter how old we are. Some birthdays are particularly special, and Clare had been thinking for weeks about her son Paul who would be sixteen that coming October. Clare had become pregnant as a virtually penniless student. Her main concern was the welfare of the baby. What could she offer at that time in her life? There seemed to be no future, no security and after much contemplation, adoption seemed the only sensible solution. Paul was adopted into a loving, comfortable home, with an older sister and an extended family who adored him. Happy and secure, he reached his sixteenth birthday unaware of Clare's continued concern and desire to know that he was well, safe and coping with life.

The birthday dawned and Clare felt compelled to find his birth certificate, tucked away so safely she couldn't remember where. She also had some adoption papers inadvertently sent to her by the adoption agency so she knew that Paul's adopted mother had the initials M. A. and his surname was Bullough. Having recently moved into a new flat in London, Clare was busy filling shelves with her many books, determined to become ship-shape as soon as possible. As she worked, the need to find Paul's birth certificate became more urgent and she frantically tried to recall where she had last seen it. Suddenly, without warning, a large hardbacked book toppled from the top shelf and hit Clare on the head with a resounding thud. Recovering from the shock she picked it up and found to her amazement it had fallen open revealing the birth certificate and adoption details of her son which had been tucked inside.

As she sat gazing at these papers she inevitably thought: 'Where is he now? Could he possibly be in London?' She reached for the telephone directories, realizing that it would be like finding the proverbial needle in a haystack. She eventually discovered an M. A. Bullough and to her astonishment the address listed was her own block of flats.

Suffice to say, a whole string of coincidences led to Clare and Paul being reunited, and they are now firm friends. It took a great deal of courage for Clare to allow me to include her story in this book, as she is a well-known actress, appearing on stage, screen and television, and until this day only her close friends have known about Paul.

Iris Gower is one of Wales's most prolific and successful writers, her books lining the shelves of city-centre bookshops everywhere. She is also a good example of my theory that people of an artistic nature experience a high incidence of synchronicity in their lives. When I discussed this with her, we agreed that this was possibly the result of being more 'spiritually open'. It may be that the sensitive and intuitive character of artistic expression leads to this type of experience. Could it even be that artists are themselves giving out something in their creative work which encourages these things to happen?

There is a theory that a community of Welsh-speaking people settled in New York State in a place now called Troy, where they intermarried with a tribe of Native Americans called the Madan. The Madan differ from most Native American tribes who are nomadic, being agriculturalists and dwelling in lodges. Highly-skilled in many artistic pursuits, they have become particularly adept as potters. So well did they integrate with the Welsh settlers that some researchers believe many Madan words are Welsh in origin.

All of this was most fascinating to Iris, and her book, *Firebird*, brings together these two cultures. The main character in the book is called Joe, a short version of a tribal name. He is half-Welsh and half-Native American Madan, very tall and extremely handsome. In addition, Iris gave him a charismatic nature and a keen interest in all things Celtic.

Research and writing were going well when Iris was chairing a week-long writers' seminar and workshop at Caerleon in Wales. Inevitably, her latest book and the character of Joe came up and were discussed. One afternoon during the course of the seminar, Iris went into the small town of Caerleon to visit the shops. Strolling around, to her delight she found a shop selling Celtic art and artefacts. She went inside, and there behind the counter stood the double of Joe, her character, in flesh and blood. He was half-Welsh, half-Native American, tall and extremely handsome. Iris also discovered, when she engaged him in conversation, that he possessed the requisite charisma too . . .

A close friend of mine was foreign correspondent for the *Sydney Morning Herald* for many years. In the spring of 1988 she was posted to London for three years. Having lived and worked all over the world, she was acquainted with many international journalists, and had two particularly interesting Swedish friends. She always looked forward to meeting up with them in various spots on the globe.

Two remarkable coincidences occurred concerning one of these Swedish journalists. He was born in a small town in the northernmost inhabited community in Sweden, so isolated the dialect was virtually a different language. One day, half a world away, this journalist was working in Japan. Needing to keep an appointment in a hurry he hailed a taxi. To his amazement, not only was the taxi-driver Swedish, but he came from the same tiny, isolated community.

Some time later my friend and I were guests at the London Barbican Centre where the Swedenborgian

Church in Britain was celebrating the tricentenary of the birth of its founder, the Swedish philosopher and theologian Swedenborg. The 'top table' was reserved for the dignitaries and the guest of honour, the former Swedish Ambassador to China. The dining-room was packed to capacity for this grand dinner and people entering the dining-room at the end of the queue were having difficulty finding a seat. I was the very last in line and to my embarrassment could not find a seat anywhere. The only empty chair in the whole dining-hall was on the top table immediately opposite the Swedish Ambassador. This, I concluded, was for some late important dignitary. At a loss as to what to do next, I was surprised to be invited to take the empty seat by the Ambassador, who assured me it was extra to requirements.

During the dinner I thought it best to keep quiet and let the dignitaries converse. Half-way through, however, a silence fell on the table. The Ambassador, searching for something to say, asked me if I had ever been to Sweden. 'No,' I replied, 'I have only ever met one Swede beside yourself in my life and that was yesterday at a friend's flat.' 'What was his name?' he asked, laughing. When I told him, his mouth fell open, for many years ago they had been close friends and colleagues on a newspaper in Sweden. The reporter had been sent abroad and they had lost touch. I was not only able to bring him up to date with his long lost friend's news, but I then introduced him to my friend (sitting on a nearby table) and she was able to put them in touch again after a twenty-year gap.

Everyone knows that children have a great affinity for art. They have no concept of what is considered 'good' or 'bad' art but they love expressing themselves. However, their creativity often takes on a different form from that which adults expect. I recall a day spent helping at my children's playgroup, when the teacher had a wonderful idea. We were to spread a huge sheet of paper on the floor, fill empty washing-up bottles with paint and pierce one or two holes in the side. Each child would have a different colour and stand around the edge of the paper and squeeze their bottles. We were told with great confidence that this would result in a spectacular splatter effect, a riot of colour and painting of great originality.

The children squeezed their bottles, saw the results and then almost simultaneously and with lightning reflexes turned the bottles on each other!

The next story begins in the Second World War when paints were limited and Maureen was attending junior school. Occasionally, on the last period of a Friday afternoon they were allowed to paint and Maureen looked forward to this session with great excitement. She freely admits that she has little artistic prowess, but loves colour and its application. One Friday afternoon, the class was told to draw a flower. It was emphasized that they should use their imagination. As Maureen was an inner-city child, dandelions and daisies were all she knew at first hand, so she settled to the project with great enthusiasm.

Eventually, the class finished their paintings and the teacher slowly walked down the aisle of desks examining the work. She came to a halt by Maureen's desk. There on the paper was a tulip-shaped heather-coloured flower, dotted and crossed with black, leaving small white squares – decidedly original. Maureen beamed with pride, thrilled with her efforts. The teacher, however, burst the bubble of happiness by telling her how stupid she was – no-one had ever seen such a flower, it was nonsense.

Crushed, Maureen walked home with the still wet painting in her hand. She had been told to use her imagination, and that flower had appeared in her head so clearly she had to paint it. The painting was pushed into a cupboard and over the years Maureen would look at it sadly until one day she threw it away and forgot all about it.

However, her appreciation of art grew, and in her late teens she would visit art galleries and exhibitions, and buy books about art and architecture. Her friend had just returned from Glasgow, a city neither had visited before, and had been most impressed by her introduction to the work of the famous Charles Rennie Mackintosh. On her coffee-table were several books illustrating his work. Maureen flicked through one, when suddenly she stopped as if turned to stone. Staring open-mouthed in disbelief, she saw her childhood flower, the exact shape, colour and design, painted by the great Mackintosh. The painting was entitled *Fritillaria* and depicted four of these beautiful flowers.

One of the things which I find most exciting and enjoyable about researching and writing a book such as this is having an idea in my head which life later confirms. As I listened with fascination to the stories related to me by actors, writers and artists, the idea entered my head that a composer or musician must surely be the most 'open' of all artistic types, yet my research had not revealed any examples. I would value an experience from a professional musician, I thought, to support the 'extra sensitive' theory.

Then 'out of the blue' I was put in touch with the composer Mike Rowland. Anyone who has practised yoga or meditation is almost certainly familiar with Mike Rowland's haunting, inspired music which induces the most stressed folk to relax. Here is a spectacular story, linked to one of his earliest and most famous compositions, *The Fairy Ring*.

Mike has always spent long periods alone in nature,

which provides inspiration for his compositions. One day he was walking alone in the grounds of Stansted Hall, when he walked into what he describes as a 'force field', within which he felt surrounded by a circle of bright lights and experienced a power so strong that the only way he can describe it is as pure love. Returning to the Hall, he sat down at the piano to translate these unusual experiences into music.

He also knew instinctively that these experiences would be very helpful when he taught meditation in his workshops. Later, he went back into the grounds of the Hall and found to his astonishment physical evidence on the grass, where the circle of lights had appeared. This reminded him of the naturally occurring phenomenon called by farmers 'the fairy ring', which gave the music its title.

Some time later, Mike was about to begin a session teaching meditation where he intended to use this special music. Before the session began he was feeling rather nervous. He went outside to collect something from his car, and was bewildered to see that the entire boot of the car was covered with a white substance that he can only describe as a 'frosting'. He thought perhaps someone had deliberately vandalized the car with paint stripper, but put the idea out of his mind and tried to calm himself in order to be able to take a session on meditation.

The music worked its magic, the session went well,

and Mike was calm and peaceful. Eventually, he returned to the car, where the 'frosting' was starting to fade. On close inspection he saw that this white substance was composed of tiny stars and crosses like snowflakes. No other car in the full car-park had such a coating, there were no trees to 'drip' any substance, and it was a warm day. He was, as you can imagine, totally mystified.

Subsequently, at another session Mike told the group about this unusual happening. Again, *The Fairy Ring* had been played and everyone was enchanted. On impulse, it was jokingly suggested they look at his car. They did so, and to everyone's amazement the car was again covered with the sparkling frosting!

He was persuaded to record this wonderful music and the tape has become a firm favourite, selling well many years later. The frosting has continued to appear on many occasions.

Christopher had entered a music competition and selected a piece of music which he hoped would be unfamiliar to most people, in particular to the judges. He decided on a lovely though difficult piece of Spanish piano music. Practising for hours each day, he soon became quite accomplished at it, though never to the point where he felt the sheet music to be unnecessary.

The day of the competition arrived and his parents

were going to drive him the two hundred miles to the venue. He was extremely nervous, changing his shirt several times until he felt completely comfortable. He put his lucky mascot, a small wooden rabbit he had owned since childhood, into his briefcase and off they went. Mentally, he began to go over various parts of the score in his head until, when they arrived, he was beginning to feel more excited than nervous. He was shown to a room behind the stage where he could prepare himself and he sat down alone to compose his thoughts.

Soon he was told that he had ten minutes before he was due on stage. He lifted the music from his case, only to find that it was the wrong music. How he could possibly have put the wrong score in his case he could not imagine, but the fact was that his little-known and beautiful Spanish piece was missing. As severe panic threatened to set in, he told himself that he knew it thoroughly and there was no reason why he could not play from memory, but this was to no avail as he felt terrified of his mind going blank out of fear. Then anger took over, and, despairing at how he could have been so stupid, he thumped the top of the piano, kicked the piano stool violently and sent it crashing over, spilling all its contents on to the floor.

Feeling ashamed at this outburst, Christopher bent to pick up the sheets of music. As he lifted them up, he stopped suddenly with his arm half-raised, as if struck by lightning. There was his piece, the Spanish music which he had believed to be so rare! Grabbing it out of the pile, he dashed to the stage, relief and incredulity flooding over him in equal measure – and won the competition. Strangely, he never did discover to whom the music belonged.

✳✳✳ 4 ✳✳✳

On the Lighter Side

'Angels can fly because they take themselves lightly.'

G. K. CHESTERTON

If you have ever doubted that humour exists in heaven, the next story will surely change your mind.

The vicar's family cat was stuck up a tree. The vicar tried every way he could think of to entice it down but the cat refused to budge. Then the vicar had an ingenious idea. He lassoed a rope to the high branch on which the cat was perched and fastened the other end to the bumper of his car. The plan was to drive forward and so bend the branch near enough to the ground either to enable someone to reach the cat or let the animal jump down. The branch, however, snapped.

At the same time as the vicar was performing this act of compassion, a neighbour and her daughter were having a tea party on the back lawn. 'Can I please have a cat, mummy?' the little girl asked for the fifteenth time that day. 'Why don't you pray to Jesus for one?' said mother, hoping to stall the child. No sooner had she spoken than a large ginger cat came hurtling through the air and landed on the picnic table. 'Thank you, Jesus,' said the little girl. The mother was speechless – that would teach her to be so glib about the power of prayer. The child was overjoyed.

Next morning in the supermarket the mother was stocking up on cat food when the vicar approached. 'I didn't know you had a cat,' he said, beginning to put two and two together. 'I didn't,' she replied, 'until yesterday. Vicar, do you believe in miracles?'

It was never going to be an ordinary wedding. Melissa had been born with the proverbial silver spoon in her mouth. Growing up in the quintessential English village, surrounded by an adoring family, her every material need catered for, she grew to expect only the best in life. She was essentially a good person, but even her nearest and dearest had to admit she was more than a little spoilt.

The wedding was to be perfection itself. Melissa had always wanted to marry at Christmas, her favourite time of year, and preparations were carried out with military precision. A team of landscape gardeners had been hired to ensure the church grounds were perfect. The church was festooned with holly, poinsettias and scarlet ribbon, and the largest

Christmas tree capable of squeezing through the church door was erected by the altar and lit with hundreds of tiny bulbs. In addition to this, each windowsill was to be illuminated by Scandinavian-style candlesticks, powered by electricity and requiring a great deal of wiring and electrical organization.

At last all was ready, the great day dawned and in mid-afternoon the horse-drawn carriage pulled up at the church. Out stepped the bride, holly in her hair, holding a bouquet and looking beautiful. To cap it all, there had been a light dusting of snow. Melissa had the perfection she had ordered.

Taking her father's arm, she stepped into the little village church, always rather dark inside, but now glowing and twinkling and smelling of pine. The organ swelled to full throttle, the congregation rose in admiration and Melissa stepped on to the rich (and newly-cleaned) carpet to proceed down the aisle.

Suddenly, they were plunged into darkness and silence. The lights all went out, the organ cut off in its prime. The unthinkable had happened and there had been a power-cut. A few old-fashioned candles were quickly lit, the piano hastily pushed from the adjoining Sunday school and pressed into action for the hymns. Everyone was shocked that all the planning had been thrown awry by the only unforeseen circumstance and strange coincidence.

Melissa was, of course, very cross, but one of the

guests was somewhat amused when she heard the vicar say in a whispered aside, 'Who says heaven hasn't a sense of humour?'

Julian lives in Sydney, Australia. One day he went into a bookshop to buy a book that turned out to be out of stock. As he walked out of the store, he caught a glimpse of a book entitled *Coincidence*. On impulse, he bought it. Having half an hour to spare, Julian went into a milk bar for a coffee and started to read the book. Ken Anderson is a Sydney-based author and the preface began, 'I first became interested in coincidences when I placed money on two horses in the Melbourne Cup which came in first and third in the race'. Julian looked at his watch, and discovered that it was not only the day but the exact time that the Melbourne Cup was being run.

A story dating to the Second World War and set in Africa demonstrates that synchronicity is worldwide. A South African woman took it upon herself to bake cakes to send to South African soldiers serving in Europe. One Christmas she baked 150 large cakes, but just before the cakes were packed she discovered to her dismay that her wedding ring was missing. Presumably it had fallen into the rich mixture and was now deep inside one of the cakes.

Not having the heart to spoil them all, she sent them

off as planned, including a note with them explaining what she thought had happened, advising the recipients to bite warily and asking that the ring should be returned if found.

The ring eventually arrived home. The soldier to whom the cake containing the ring had been allocated was her own son!

A young woman was about to travel from Los Angeles to London for a three-month holiday with friends during her summer break from university. Her next-door neighbour in Los Angeles, an old lady of eighty-eight years and originally a Londoner, was very interested and enjoyed hearing all of her plans. This woman, although kind and pleasant enough, was a little 'dotty'. Shortly before her friend was to leave for London, the old lady handed her a letter she had painstakingly written to an old friend in London. She had not contacted this friend for some forty years, did not know the address and had simply written on the envelope 'To Martha White, London'.

Her friend smiled, knowing London possessed at least six million inhabitants and thinking that the woman in question was probably long departed. Nevertheless she took the letter and pushed it into her anorak pocket, not wishing to upset the old lady.

After a week or two in London, she found herself with a free day to explore alone for the first time. She set out for a walk and presently came to an area with several antique shops. As she browsed she suddenly became aware of an old lady by her side. They had both been admiring the same item. They fell into conversation and the old lady observed that she was chatting to an American and asked where she was from. When she was told LA, she said, 'I had a friend who went to live in LA many years ago, although I imagine she has passed away by now. Allow me to introduce myself – my name is Martha White.' After the initial shock, the young woman reached into her anorak pocket. 'Believe it or not,' she said, 'I have a letter for you!'

A humorous story related by Ken Anderson is connected with a manuscript.

One Friday night early in 1992, a London publisher was dining in a Notting Hill Gate restaurant when thieves broke into her car. Amongst the things stolen was a manuscript she had high hopes for, although she had not yet told its author. This loss upset her most about the incident. The thieves, however, did not think as highly of the manuscript and, unknown to her, threw it over a wall.

She spent a nervous weekend and in her office on Monday morning was trying to decide how she should deal with the problem when a call came from the author of the manuscript. In a voice tinged more with sorrow than anger he asked the publisher: 'Why did you have my manuscript thrown over my front wall?'

The next few stories should perhaps be described as gravely humorous.

Canadian actor Charles Coghlan became ill and died in Galverstone, Texas, during a tour of the American state in 1899. He was buried in a lead coffin which was sealed inside a vault.

In September 1900, less than a year after his burial, a rainstorm hit Galverstone, flooding the cemetery and breaking open the vault. Coghlan's coffin floated away, into the Gulf of Mexico, then drifted along the Florida coastline out into the Atlantic, where the Gulf Stream took over and carried it north.

One day in 1908, some fishermen on Prince Edward Island, Canada, saw a long, weather-beaten box floating ashore – Coghlan's coffin. The actor's body had floated more than 5,600 kilometres – to his home! His fellow islanders reburied him in the grave-yard of the church where he had been baptised.

Funerals, I'm sure you will agree, are not normally occasions for humour, even if families often join together in a meal afterwards and laugh from the release of tension and emotion. I recall a family funeral where an uncle of mine performed Charlie Chaplin impressions and had everyone in stitches.

The funeral in my next story, however, was particularly sad. Heather had died after a bitter struggle with motor neurone disease. A bright, independent, professional lady, she possessed a sharp sense of humour and had led a very active life. It was a particularly cruel blow when she found speech difficult and she could no longer make herself understood. Despite this obstacle, the old wit and humour would shine through and a glimpse of her vitality appear.

Finally, her only child, Mary, was forced to admit her mother needed twenty-four-hour nursing care and agreed to the doctor's recommendation that Heather should enter a nursing home. A good nursing home was found and Heather moved into a bright room with a patio and pleasant view. Mary, determined to make the surroundings as attractive as possible, went to the garden centre and bought lots of brightly coloured plants to place in tubs on the patio. Unfortunately, the disease was progressing very rapidly and only a short time after Heather had entered the nursing home she died.

The funeral was moving and dignified. A large congregation attended to pay their respects, and Mary felt a sense of peace mingled with the loss. Several close family members had travelled hundreds of miles to attend and they planned to stay the night with Mary before driving home the following day. The next morning dawned bright and crisp and Heather's sister expressed a desire to see again the grounds of the crematorium and the small patch of ground where Heather's ashes would be scattered. Mary decided to take the plants she had bought for the patio and place them around the ground beside the little plaque bearing Heather's name.

They arrived early at the crematorium to allow time for the family to see the grounds and the plot before driving the long journey home. After some time searching they found the little plot with Heather's plaque and Mary started to plant the flowers. It had obviously been hastily prepared, the grass was covered with dirt and grit, so before Mary could plant she took her trowel and scraped away as much dirt as possible on to the path.

All was finished and the little patch of ground looked lovely, a fitting tribute to Heather. They had one last look around and walked slowly back to the car-park. When she looked at other newly laid patches of grass on their way, a bell began to ring in Mary's head. The truth hit her – the dirt she had scraped from the grass was in fact her mother's ashes, now strewn on the path! Despite the shock, Mary could do nothing but laugh. She felt sure her mother could see the funny side and was chuckling in heaven.

For years, Diane and Rachel had been close friends. Humour was the lynch-pin of this friendship, and they never failed to make each other laugh. Rachel had a very dry, sometimes almost black sense of humour, and was a great 'character'.

One Christmas, Rachel, who was unmarried and without children, spent the holiday with Diane. Diane's two daughters, Jenny and Sarah, were thrilled with the delightful presents she gave them, particularly a toy dog containing batteries. When switched on, it would react to a voice by barking.

Although that Christmas was a happy one there was a shadow hanging over the festivities, for Rachel was suffering from terminal cancer. Just three months later Diane lost her close and courageous friend, who had retained her sense of humour to the very end of her life and could still make Diane laugh.

The year rolled on to the next Christmas. On Christmas Eve, while the girls were in bed fast asleep, Diane quietly completed the last task of the busy day, ironing the girls' dresses for church on Christmas morning. The house was completely silent and her thoughts turned to Rachel. She had missed her very much that year and she found herself saying silently, 'Hope you are happy, Rachel' and sending her their love.

Suddenly, Diane jumped almost out of her skin as the toy dog Rachel had given the children last Christmas started to bark. The toy was in a box, under the bed, had not been played with for some time, and no voice had activated it. Diane could scarcely believe her ears, but pondering this event later, she decided that if Rachel had wanted to contact her, this would be exactly the way she would do it – to make Diane laugh!

*** 5 ***

Dreams and Symbols

'Dreams are true while they last, and do we not live in dreams?'

ALFRED, LORD TENNYSON

We have seen how universal coincidences are, and this is also true of dreams. We all dream and it is likely that many of us are aware of the power of the symbols in our dreams.

Aborigines and Native Americans regard dreaming as another level of awareness and they place great importance on the 'dream catcher', which was mentioned in the introduction. It is a web-like structure woven with brightly coloured threads and hung behind one's head at night to help one remember and 'catch' the dream. Real spiders' webs are also used in this way. Ceremonies feature these objects asking superhuman powers to assist in unlocking the message of a dream. The great spirit of the universe is invoked to give answers in dreams. Should these people have any health problems, relationship troubles, or even problems understanding life's experiences, it is firmly believed dreams can provide an answer. Spiritual messages, warnings, predictions, all are evident in dreams, and the belief is that they mirror reality. Dream catchers then are essential symbols for these people, the web mirroring all aspects of their lives, interlaced and circular.

Dreams can also yield meaning to modern-day Westerners. They may convey optimism or a warning. As an example of the latter, when watching television some time ago I saw a programme about an archaeological dig. The so-called 'Ice Maiden' was a princess from the Pazyryk tribe, who had been preserved in ice in the colder reaches of Mongolia for 2,500 years. One member of the team revealed that during the dig, led by a Russian archaeologist, the entire group suffered from disturbing and horrific dreams. She felt that the message was that the body should be left in peace in its resting-place.

Dreams and coincidences are often closely interwoven as Carl Jung discovered through his interest in dreams as well as his psychological research concerning coincidence. Analysing dreams was a powerful tool in helping his patients to make progress.

One of the best-known stories told about Jung and his developing theory of synchronicity concerned a patient who was visiting him and making little progress. During one appointment, she told him of a vivid dream she'd had the previous night. She had dreamt of a scarab beetle. As she began to relate this dream there was a tapping at the window. Jung opened it, and discovered an insect very closely related to the scarab beetle making the tapping noise. The insect fitted her description almost exactly. The woman was quite shocked by this incident, and Jung realized that it was extremely important. It shook her out of her normal way of thinking and helped her to make progress.

Jung read great symbolism into the tapping on the window: an example of synchronicity, which prompted the opening of the window and the opening of the woman's mind. Deeper meaning still, however, can be attached to this, for Jung knew that in Egyptian culture, the scarab plays a significant role and is the symbol of rebirth. Freud's original idea of the unconscious was much extended by Jung, because he saw it as the source of these symbols which can help in our development, but, ultimately, how meaningful the coincidence or symbolism is depends on whether or not the individual chooses to see its meaning.

DREAM MESSAGES

For one young woman in Australia, a dream and a seemingly unrelated incident now appear inextricably linked and convey an important message.

Susan normally has difficulty remembering dreams, other than unrelated images. This time, however, the dream was remarkably vivid. She was at the top of an enormous tree, so high and with such thick foliage she could not see the ground. Standing on a thick limb of this tree she was conscious that two figures were standing on either side of her. To the right was a tall man, with dark, shoulder-length hair, dressed in a robe. She knew this was a spiritual figure. A sense of quiet strength, peace and authority emanated from him. The other figure was less clear but she believes it was also dressed in a robe.

Enormous though this branch was, she felt it start to break and her thoughts were that a fall so far from the ground must surely be fatal. Instantly, to her surprise, she found herself and the two figures standing on solid ground at the base of the tree, totally uninjured. She asked the smiling figure, 'Why have we not been killed?' His response was a look that beamed pure love.

Trying to interpret this dream it seemed to Susan that it symbolized her life. So often she had been out on a limb and in need of help and protection. Could this dream be saying 'You are not alone, the comfort and help you need are there for you'?

The following day Susan related the dream to her mother, who listened quietly and then told her daughter of an incident that had happened the previous day, immediately before Susan's dream. Susan's mother had been driving through a small town some thirty minutes by car from Susan's house. She saw a young hitchhiker, and offered her a lift. They chatted with an instant rapport and the girl revealed that she was staying at a retreat but needed to visit the local shops in the next small town. The girl had at some point suffered from some form of paralysis but had received spiritual healing and was now well. She was a Christian and told Susan's mother how very powerful she thought prayer to be and how vital it was to the life of the retreat.

They reached the small town and Susan's mother offered to wait for her to complete her shopping and drive her back to the retreat. They had both enjoyed each other's company and it was one of those chance encounters that led one to wonder if there was a reason for it. The girl left the car and thanked Susan's mother for her help. Just before she walked away she announced that she would 'pray in the retreat for your daughter'. That night Susan had the dream. She concludes that the dream was confirmation that help from a high source was there for her.

Coincidence and dreams are sometimes related but the meaning is not always clear. Wendy has tried to find meaning or symbolism in her experience but has to date been unsuccessful. Some form of telepathy has been suggested but the time-scale between events would lead one to doubt that explanation.

Ireland had always held a fascination for Wendy, so when a friend proposed a five-day trip in spring on a bargain fly/drive break, she agreed with enthusiasm.

One night in January before the holiday Wendy had a strange dream. It did not make any sense to her, but it was sharply vivid. On waking it seemed so real she could not get it out of her mind. In this dream she was driving along a country lane looking for somewhere to eat. For miles there did not seem to be any buildings, just green fields and hedges. Eventually, she saw a large sign saying 'Restaurant' with a large gold painted arrow. Turning off the main lane she followed the direction indicated by the arrow. Presently, the lane widened and she drove into a large car-park immediately in front of a large, splendid house, covered with ivy with two large coach lamps on either side of the green door.

Stepping inside, she found herself in an elegant hall with a reception desk and a smiling receptionist dressed in a red jacket. Wendy asked for a table for lunch, but the lady said apologetically that the restaurant was fully booked and could not provide her with a meal. At this point, a waiter dressed in white appeared and announced that they could accommodate her since they had opened a lounge and turned it into an extra dining room. Asking her to follow, he set off down a long corridor, thickly carpeted in red and gold. The small lounge was beautiful and she vividly recalls an enormous fireplace and above the mantel the biggest stuffed fish one could imagine, in a glass case.

Wendy woke totally bemused but fascinated by the detail and colour she could recall, for mostly she could not remember her dreams.

The months passed and eventually the holiday departure date arrived. On the third day in Ireland they drove along, soaking up the scenery, keen not to rush. By 1 p.m. they were very hungry, but after several miles there was no sign of anywhere to eat. Suddenly Wendy's friend pointed out a sign at the side of the road which simply said 'Restaurant'. 'There,' she said, 'let's try this.' Wendy looked up in disbelief. The sign had a large gold arrow pointing down the lane. The lane opened up into a car-park, the large house was covered with ivy, and so it went on; she was actually living her dream.

The receptionist, who was dressed in a red jacket, said the exact words, 'We have no table vacant.' A white-coated waiter said, 'Follow me' and they walked down the red and gold carpeted corridor to the small lounge. Wendy was shaking as she entered the room, for there was the huge fireplace and above it the enormous stuffed fish in a glass case. She had lived her dream exactly, colours, objects, sequence of events, every detail. She had never visited the country before and is totally baffled by the whole episode.

An eightieth birthday is a special event, and Henrietta's family planned to make it a day to remember. A family party was planned at an elegant restaurant and family members were travelling from near and far for the occasion. None would be travelling further than Florence, Henrietta's sister, who would be arriving from Canada. Florence, a mere seventy-eight, thought nothing of hopping on a plane for this special occasion. It would be ten years since her last visit, and everyone involved was looking forward to the reunion.

The night before the big day Henrietta had a dream. She saw Florence on the aeroplane, smiling and holding a huge bunch of flowers. Waking suddenly, Henrietta sat up in bed. It was only 1 a.m., she felt very restless and had a great deal of trouble getting back to sleep. This, she thought, was due to the excitement building for the following day.

The next evening she was driven by her son and his family to the restaurant. Assembled there were forty friends and family, music playing to make a very happy atmosphere. The only problem was that Florence had not arrived. Henrietta's son told her that the plane had been delayed. There was nothing for it but to go ahead with the meal. Henrietta couldn't remember enjoying an evening more, and when she eventually arrived home she was exhausted, slept soundly and did not wake until quite late the following morning.

Making a pot of tea in the kitchen she saw her son and daughter-in-law coming up the garden path. They all sat down for a cup of tea and she thanked them for all the hard work they had put in arranging the day. There was still no word from Florence, she realized, and she decided she would ring and find out exactly what had happened. Her son gently said, 'No need, Mum, we knew and didn't want to tell you yesterday and spoil the celebrations, but Florence has died.'

The shock and sadness were hard to cope with but when Henrietta had been given all the details and they worked out the time difference, it emerged that Florence had died on the night before the party, at 1 a.m. to be precise.

Jane's mother was renowned throughout her family and circle of friends for her lack of geographical knowledge. Everyone knew that when Jane announced she was going to live and work in America her mother would have virtually no idea where in the world her daughter would be. Undeterred, Jane set forth promising to be closely in touch at all times. True to her promise, beautiful cards, photographs and letters arrived thick and fast from San Francisco. Her mother started to enjoy geography at last.

One night, Jane's mother had an incredibly vivid

dream. She saw her daughter in a desert setting, surrounded by palm trees and deep blue skies. Jane told her mother in the dream that this was Palm Springs, a beautiful desert town. On waking, Jane's mother turned to her husband and told him of this strikingly clear dream. 'Is there a place called Palm Springs?' she asked. He had no idea. As she went downstairs to start making breakfast she was aware of the postman walking up the path, followed by a slam of the letter-box as a postcard was pushed through. She bent and picked it up from the hall mat, scarcely able to believe her eyes as she saw it was a postcard from Palm Springs in the Mojave desert! Her daughter was on holiday there, but her mother had never heard the name before in her entire life.

A friend recently told me about a dream she'd had in which she stood in a hospital room. The dream was remarkably vivid and every detail could be recalled – the furniture and furnishings, even an open cupboard with white towels stacked neatly inside. She found the dream slightly unnerving, it was so very clear in her mind. The following day she heard that a close relative had been taken into hospital seriously ill. The news gave her goosebumps, she said.

Shortly after being told this story, I heard a very similar event had happened elsewhere. A young woman also dreamt of a hospital scene, seeing an ambulance arrive outside the hospital, lights flashing and siren sounding. She saw doctors and nurses rush the patient on a trolley into an operating theatre. On waking she could recall every detail. She told her parents at breakfast and her father laughed, accusing her of watching too many hospital dramas on television.

At six o'clock that evening they received a telephone call from the local hospital saying her father had fallen from his motorbike, having lost control on an icy patch, and was in surgery having a badly damaged leg attended to.

THE POWER OF SYMBOLS

I have already mentioned the power of symbols in connection with dreams, but they are by no means restricted to dreams, of course. Do any of us fully realize, I wonder, just how powerful symbols are in our lives and how they link us to past generations? Ancient myths involving symbols have passed from generation to generation and are incorporated into evolving lifestyles and festivals. Civilizations are rather like children who are open to all sorts of mystical and imaginary experiences. As they grow, however, this aspect of their nature is subjugated. Civilizations behave similarly, their so-called sophistication blocking out the meanings of symbols yet retaining a vestige of the wisdom.

Looking at tribal cultures and the ways of indigenous peoples, we can see the undiluted wisdom linking Nature, lifestyle and spirituality into a whole. Symbols play a powerful part in their lives, and influence how decisions are made. They are found in many forms of divination, ritual, mythology and art.

Are symbols equally important to people in the Western world as we approach the millennium? Have science and technology replaced mysticism and symbolism? It is my belief that symbols are as powerful and meaningful as ever. Many festivals continue evoking the legends and myths surrounding spring and new birth. Easter eggs dominate every household in spring also, a very ancient symbol of new life. They have been incorporated into the Christian calendar and integrated with the story of Christ's rising from the dead, symbolizing new life and new hope. Christmas also incorporates ancient winter festivals into Christianity. Mistletoe, yule logs and other pagan elements mingle with the star and angels.

Personal symbols also affect our lives greatly. I was talking to a woman recently who had lost her husband in an industrial accident. The shock was enormous and all she could feel was numbness. The funeral and all the surrounding family business did not bring a tear; it was as if she had turned into ice. Family, friends and her GP were all worried, realizing the importance of 'letting go'. Time passed and the difficult task of disposing of personal effects had to be tackled, but still the numbness held sway.

What finally melted the ice was a simple key ring. On a special holiday, years ago, she had bought her husband a key ring in the form of a Celtic cross embossed on a leather fob. He had loved it and carried it with him at all times. It held the keys to the house, their holiday cottage, his car, his office, the garden shed containing tools and the children's bikes – in short, his entire life was represented on that one key ring. The symbolism then opened the floodgates and she could at last cry.

The next two stories involve flowers. There is a wealth of symbolism associated with flowers. For example, they remind us of love (roses), death (lilies), marriage (orange blossom). What is more, every conceivable occasion in our lives may be marked with a bouquet of flowers – birth, birthdays, christenings, weddings and funerals to name but a few.

There are few things in life which lift the spirits more than flowers, especially in the early spring, when it is exhilarating after a long winter to see the crocuses and daffodils appear expressing hope and new life. It's little wonder that Wordsworth's most famous poem is the one which he was moved to write at the sight of daffodils in spring.

Audrey's mother was a florist and as far back as she

can remember Audrey was surrounded by beautiful sights and fragrances. It was difficult for her to choose a favourite flower, but her mother preferred violets for their gloriously rich colour, their dainty appearance and lovely scent.

Audrey never saw a violet without thinking of her mother. She gave them to her each Mothering Sunday and far from thinking them 'coals to Newcastle' her mother was always delighted. Over the years, Audrey's mother received many items of a violet colour. Even birthday cards would often feature them and frequently she would wear the colour also.

Years passed and one day, without warning, Audrey's mother collapsed, falling to the floor in great pain. Without delay, an ambulance was called and she was rushed to the nearest hospital. A heart attack was diagnosed immediately on arrival and she was rushed into intensive care. Audrey and other members of the family waited outside in a state of shock, for her mother was still a fairly young woman, having suffered a heart attack at forty-eight years old. Sadly, after only a short time, Audrey's mother died. She was removed to a small side-room, where Audrey and her family could sit with her for a time while the awful truth sank in. It was so difficult to comprehend and when they stood up to leave it was as if they moved in some awful nightmare.

Audrey stood at the door of the little room, bare

except for the bed and a few chairs. Tears streaming down her face, she blew her mother a kiss. Instantly, the room was filled with the scent of violets. Audrey could scarcely believe it. How could that possibly be? There were no flowers to be seen anywhere. She asked a nurse if she had recently removed flowers from the room. 'No,' she replied, 'but I have to say that it's not the first time this has happened . . .'

When Audrey told me this story, I was able to add that when researching *An Angel at my Shoulder* I had been told a very similar story by a man visiting his mother in hospital where the staff also confirmed that it was not the first time that the intense perfume of violets had pervaded the room when someone died. 'Perhaps violets are the scent of angels,' Audrey replied, 'coming to take her to heaven.'

Our next story also involves a beautiful flower and here too it was central to a person's state of mind at a certain point in his life. A friend of mine was going through a very bad patch in life, confused about his choice of career and under strain emotionally from all directions. He decided to take the advice of a friend and see a counsellor, which helped. He also planned a short walking holiday with his girlfriend, knowing that the countryside always made him feel better and recharged his batteries.

Just before going on holiday, he visited his

counsellor again and this time articulated his feelings using the analogy of a flower. His life felt dark and dank like the roots in muddy water, but he was striving to grow towards the light. The counsellor encouraged him to put the image down on paper and he later did so using a pad and pencils. When he packed his rucksack for the holiday, he put the pad into one of the pockets, thinking he might try to draw whilst in the countryside.

On the second day of the holiday my friend and his companion decided on a picnic and set off across the fields. The land became undulating and then a little steeper and presently they approached a large dry-stone wall, with steps to climb up and over into the next field. My friend climbed first, but on reaching the top gasped in astonishment. Turning to his girlfriend he said, 'Before you climb the steps there is something I must show you.' He took the drawing pad from his rucksack and handed it to her. He had drawn a yellow iris, very well indeed, surprising in itself because he would be the first to admit artistic prowess was not one of his talents. His girlfriend admired the drawing and then followed the steps to the top of the wall where she too gasped, for there was a field full of wild yellow irises!

Not long after the holiday my friend was looking for a birthday gift for his girlfriend. Pottering around a village he did not know whilst waiting for a train, he came across a gift shop and there in the front of the window was a pretty brooch, depicting a bunch of yellow irises.

Chris is the editor of a magazine, always busy, always trying to meet deadlines, juggle finances and produce a first-class edition of his magazine. Like most people, his work was sometimes a pleasure to him and sometimes a great worry. One winter had been a particular struggle, and things seemed to go wrong for weeks. Every aspect of the job seemed a chore and he longed for it all to run smoothly.

One night, long after he would normally have finished, he was wrestling with a particular problem and feeling very weary. Glancing up, he saw the snow had started to fall, swirling past the window, beautiful against the dark sky. It was already covering the courtyard and Chris felt he must be on his way before it became a problem. Switching off the light with a heavy heart, he muttered aloud, 'If my angel is listening, please help.'

The cold hit his face as he closed the front door and made his way across the cobbled square to his car. Everything looked beautiful, the trees like filigree work and the cobbles almost completely obliterated by the delicate flakes. Taking the key from his pocket, Chris bent to insert it in the car lock. Suddenly something caught his eye, almost buried in the snow, yet twinkling in the street lamp's glow. He bent to pick it up and to his amazement found in the palm of his hand a little golden angel. Wonderment, hope and a belief that all would be well filled his heart. He knew he simply had to trust.

This story is set in Australia and concerns a wonderful little girl of six years old called Genevieve. The events surrounding her short life contain an amazing coincidence, powerful symbolism and the miracle which is Genevieve herself. Her life and personality had such an impact on her family and all who came into contact with her that one can only marvel.

Genevieve was born with all the odds stacked against her, in the sense that she would never enjoy good health as other children, never be strong enough to walk or run. Physically fragile, there would be many operations and medical procedures to endure. As a Down's Syndrome baby, speech was difficult and this meant communication was not always easy. Her mother, Jeannie, told me that even odd words were rare. Destined to be ill for all of the six years of her life, one might expect Genevieve to have been depressed and difficult, but just the opposite was true. Laughter and smiles surrounded her and this happiness was infectious and spread to all around her. She brought tremendous joy to everyone she met, especially her family. Her sisters, Amy and Heather, loved her dearly and there was a tremendous bond of love between the three girls.

One of the main delights in Genevieve's life was balloons – she adored them! They held endless fascination for her, and tied to her cot in the hospital they brought her such pleasure that she never tired of them.

September of 1996 was to be a difficult time for everyone, as Genevieve's condition worsened dramatically, with complications concerning her heart and lungs draining the little girl's resources. She was, however, her courageous self, and her parents sat by her hospital cot marvelling at the spirit of their wonderful daughter. Trying to amuse her, they were colouring a picture and going through the colours of the crayons. Genevieve responded with interest as her mother, not really expecting an answer, asked her what colour of crayon she would like her to use. Swift and sure came the reply 'yellow'. Her parents were astonished, for not only were words few and far between, but often not terribly clear or distinct. Yellow was said with such emphasis they were sure that it must be her favourite colour.

That particular word and the colour concerned will continue to be of great significance and importance to all who loved Genevieve, for 'yellow' was the last word she said. On the third of September, Genevieve died, two months short of her seventh birthday, and the loss was deeply felt.

Jeannie and Paul, her devoted parents, along with the rest of the family, wanted Genevieve's funeral to celebrate her life and not simply mourn her death. The bright, happy, positive nature of their daughter had to be a strong element in the service. A devout Christian family, they believed Genevieve was now happy and free and all her suffering over. It was a time for hope, and, in Jeannie's own words, 'belief and relief'.

Yellow was to feature strongly on the day of the funeral, the colour of life and hope illustrating the sun which shone from Genevieve and warmed all who were near her. An order of service was printed on yellow paper and wonderfully headed 'The Graduation Service of Genevieve Helen Humphreys', a lovely, positive approach to loss. A close family friend wrote a beautiful and moving poem and all the flowers were bright yellow. Most moving of all was the marvellous idea of filling the church with yellow balloons. As the service came to a close, each mourner took a balloon and followed the tiny casket outside, where everyone simultaneously let go of the string of their balloon. The vision of those beautiful balloons symbolizing Genevieve's spirit soaring to heaven must have had quite an impact in itself, but, what is more, having been released from random positions on the lawn in front of the church, the balloons formed a huge cross in the sky.

Everyone watched as the balloons disappeared and

Heather said, 'Goodbye, Genevieve' to her sister. Slowly, people made their way back inside the church premises for refreshments, but Jeannie felt the need to be alone for a little while. As she gazed into the sky there appeared a magnificent rainbow.

The anniversary of Genevieve's birthday was not going to be easy. November the 18th dawned, and again Jeannie felt the need to be alone. Early in the morning she went for a long walk. Looking up suddenly, she saw another rainbow and tells me she accepted it as a lovely gift from God.

However short the life that little girl had, she also had a powerful effect on many people, with the happiness and love she radiated, and her very personality, symbolized in the colour of life. I know that I shall never be able to look at a yellow balloon without thinking of this little girl whom I never met, and of the love which she gave. I am sure that none of us who know her story will see yellow balloons in the same way again. In this fashion, Genevieve's love is literally spreading around the globe, and that's the miracle!

Humans have looked to the heavens for signs and symbols from time immemorial. Few people could fail to be moved by the sight of a star-filled sky. Christians place significance in the star which led the wise men to Bethlehem. Mariners owed their very lives to the stars before modern-day technology, and their reference points are still valued today. We may laugh at horoscopes in newspapers and magazines, but most of us read them nevertheless, and our own birth sign holds great significance for us. Science has proved that the moon affects the tides on earth, so should the stars of our birth not dramatically affect people?

Nature speaks to us with natural signs such as rainbows, which may also carry symbolic significance. The timing of these events may be crucial. One day we may see a natural phenomenon and think it merely a thing of beauty; another time, when anxious or distressed, it can be a powerful symbol of hope. The next story tells of an uplifting and life-changing event in Susan's life.

Susan has always had trust in her inner feelings. She has followed this inner guidance and always found it to be correct and positive.

Just a few years ago, Susan's life was falling apart. Physically she was undergoing tests for worrying symptoms, and mentally she was battling with the anguish of a marriage which seemed to be on the rocks. Understandably, she was very depressed. She had been forced to leave the job she loved because in her state it was far too demanding and just a simple daily routine was a huge effort. She felt helpless and hopeless despite a loving family. No-one, it seemed, could reach through the encroaching darkness.

One night, Susan felt she had reached her lowest point. All she really wanted was to die. Alone, she stepped out into the garden, steeped in despair. The night was as black as her soul and a strong wind blew thick black clouds across the sky, mirroring her inward feelings. All seemed lost. She stared up at the gloomy sky and uttered the plaintive words: 'Please, are things ever going to get better?' She wasn't at all sure whom she was addressing, but she gazed intently at the sky.

Instantly, the clouds started to part, revealing the most breathtakingly beautiful full moon Susan had ever seen. The moon's rays shone directly on to her, bathing her in calming light. Feelings of despair and depression disappeared as if by magic and she was enveloped in peace and calm. The clouds had at this point formed a circle around the moon and she stood mesmerized, knowing this was indeed a spiritual experience.

Eventually, the clouds completely covered the moon once more and Susan remembers saying 'thank you' out loud. It has had a continuing, profound effect, and slowly her life is being rebuilt.

The moon in the previous story was highly symbolic and a natural source of light. Our next story however involves light of a more mundane nature – electric light. David had trained for many years to attain his qualifications in engineering at the Technical Institute in the Czech Republic. A high achiever, David had graduated with flying colours and looked forward to a career as a water engineer.

The day arrived for his graduation ceremony. The hall was packed with proud parents and friends, and hundreds of nervous, excited graduates-to-be. Speeches were made by academic worthies, and then one by one the students went forward to receive their awards. David waited eagerly until at last his name was called. He heard the applause as he reached the platform and shook hands with the presenters. Suddenly, as he was receiving his diploma, the hall was plunged into darkness and he had to stumble in the pitch black back to his seat. Only seconds passed, but it seemed much longer, until power was restored and the ceremony resumed.

David, however, was a religious and deep-thinking person and began to interpret this experience as a sign. He was the only graduate to have been plunged into darkness. Could this mean that he was on the wrong path? Perhaps he was being told that engineering was not the way for him to go? He felt uneasy and curious and thought long and hard about the implications of this sign.

Some years later, after the Czech Revolution, David was surprised and delighted to be invited to study theology in England. He accepted with a great feeling of finding the right path and in 1995 was ordained as a minister to work in the Czech Republic. He says at last he felt his feet were travelling down the right path and he is certain that the incident at his graduation was indeed a message from a higher source than the National Grid!

The next story features rainbows in connection with most unusual meteorological conditions.

It had been a glorious day, not perhaps the best walking weather, far too hot in fact, but John and his brother had thoroughly enjoyed it despite the heat. In Wales on holiday, they decided to tackle the mountain area known as the Snowdon Horseshoe. The date was 21 June, so they took advantage of the long hours of light, and did not start to descend until late in the evening. It must have been around eight o'clock as they approached a valley with the sun directly behind them. The sky was deep blue, but the valley was filled with a light, swirling mist.

Suddenly, to their amazement, projected on to the sky was a huge figure with a rainbow circling its head, totally unlike anything they had ever encountered in life before. John then discovered on raising his arm that the figure also raised its arm, and realized it was his own reflection projected on to the backdrop of the sky. Amazed, they descended, moved and elated by the experience, and it then transpired that there had been two figures, one for each of them, but they could each only see their own figure. Each figure had a rainbow halo around its head.

When they arrived home they started to research the phenomenon and discovered it was an extremely rare meteorological condition, documented chiefly in the Himalayas, but not Snowdon, called the Brocken Spectre. John has a photograph he took of the phenomenon. Even though it could be explained scientifically, it was a powerful spiritual experience which had a lasting effect on John's life and was of great significance for him.

Nature, solid objects, mythical objects, are all rich in symbolism, but what of food and drink, staples of our very life? Bread, water and wine have a special meaning for Christians. On a more secular note, there are many British pubs called The Staff of Life. Traditionally, the last sheath of the harvest was left for the birds as a 'thank you' to Mother Earth for her bounteousness. The expression 'manna from heaven' originates from the biblical story with its life-saving symbolism. In Judaism unleavened bread is eaten at Passover for eight days as a reminder of the time when Hebrew slaves fled the serfdom of Egypt. Leaving in haste they took with them the bread which had not had sufficient time to rise. To this day the event is celebrated and on the first night of Passover the woman of the house takes a piece of the bread and sets it aside, reminding everyone of God's goodness and the belief that all things come from Him.

117

Bread is central to our next story, a strange tale that no-one involved in can begin to offer an explanation for. A young woman was asked by her two friends if she would keep an eye on their house whilst they were on holiday. Happy to oblige, she readily agreed. On the morning of their departure they called with the key and asked for one more small favour: would she please leave a loaf of bread and a pint of milk for them in the kitchen for their return? No problem, she replied.

The week went by swiftly, and the woman enjoyed a full and busy week. Saturday arrived, which was the one clear day all week. She was going to enjoy the rest and peace. Sleeping late, she leisurely read the paper, took her dog for a long walk and visited friends.

At about 5 p.m. the phone rang. It was her friends back from holiday thanking her for the loaf and milk. She went cold and was momentarily struck dumb. So busy had her week been, she had totally forgotten her friend's house and request. She certainly had not left the bread and milk. She rushed round to confess all, handing them their spare key. She asked if anyone else had been given one. The reply was that they only had two sets of keys, one they had taken away with them and she had the other set. There was no sign of forced entry, all doors and windows were locked exactly as they had been left, and yet there, large as life on the kitchen table, they had found a freshly baked loaf and a pint of milk — a puzzle they still have not solved two years later!

Perhaps the most common symbol is the circle. We often speak of the cycle of the year. Ancient people erected stone circles, modern people are perplexed by crop circles. The symbol for eternity is two rings placed on their sides. We dance in circles seeing the importance and flow of energy when all the circle members hold hands. There is a church in Edinburgh which is circular in design so that the devil could not hide in its corners. Aztecs and Incas worshipped the sun and in ancient Britain medicinal herbs were gathered by moonlight for extra properties imbued by the silver circle in the sky. Abstract mandalas are also depicted in the Christian tradition, for example the famous 'rose windows' of Chartres. Cities have sometimes been built in a circular pattern.

I was recently given a copy of an extraordinary book entitled *Mutant Message Down Under* by Marlo Morgan. It is a fictional story, but full of the wisdom of Australian Aborigines. One striking difference between us and these ancient peoples is how they conceive of time. We in modern societies are bound by clock watching, our lives are tabled by the hours, and we have generally lost the ability simply to 'be', to relax and forget about the march of the hours. Somehow coincidences have a very different sense of time, for they can bring together in a moment elements which seem to cross large swathes of 'clock-time'. We may almost feel that coincidences are moments outside time.

Circles in the form of rings are of great personal importance. Rings are exchanged on many occasions and hold a variety of meanings. Wedding rings, friendship rings, signet rings, to name just a few, give meaning to our feelings, whilst the stones embedded in them add even more significance. Stones, rings and time are all instrumental in the next story, one of my most powerful personal experiences of synchronicity.

When I was young, and my mother was only just approaching mid-life, she died very suddenly. The shock for my father and me was profound, and having no siblings to share the grief with was an additional sorrow for me. After the funeral, as always on these occasions, there were practical matters to be attended to, the disposal of personal effects being particularly painful. This task was made more harrowing by the fact that we could not find my mother's personal rings – wedding ring, engagement ring and an antique dress ring belonging to my father. We believed they were usually kept together in a small leather purse but this was not to be found anywhere. Every nook and cranny was searched and yet the rings, both financially and emotionally precious, could not be found.

Time passed and my father too died; the house was sold and stripped bare and still no sign of the rings. I had accepted at this point they were lost for ever. Twenty-five years elapsed, my daughters grew up, and from time to time I still felt the sadness descend on me as I pondered how my mother would have enjoyed seeing my daughters wear the rings.

One day I was talking to a very new friend. She was warm and perceptive and I felt at ease and close to her even after such a brief acquaintance. She was part of a very large family in contrast to myself. I told her I was an only child and my parents had died many years previously. She nodded wisely and then said, 'Time really cannot separate you, however, and I feel sure there will be some message for you shortly.'

Only a few days later, I received a phone call from a cousin of mine. This was an unexpected event, as it had been many years since we had met or even talked on the phone. 'I have some news for you,' she said. Recently she had been determined to clear out her attic. This had decades of accumulated items, and amongst the items placed on a pile labelled 'throw away' was a small sewing basket. My cousin's daughter decided to investigate and laughed at the ancient patterns inside the box. On impulse, she turned the box upside down, spilling its contents on to the floor, and there twinkling up at her were the three rings.

My cousin could scarcely believe it. She explained to me that after my mother's death my father had given little keepsakes to various members of the family. Knowing my cousin enjoyed sewing, he gave her the small work basket. For reasons we shall never know my mother kept the rings there. The basket had never been used and was eventually relegated to the attic.

After twenty-five years, I was again reunited with the precious rings and all the associated memories. Time really could not erase the love in those objects and my friend's words came to mind most forcefully: 'They are close, there will be a message'!

✳✳✴ 6 ✴✳✳

Modern-day Miracles

'There are only two ways to live your life. One is as though nothing is a miracle. The other is as though everything is a miracle.'

ALBERT EINSTEIN

It is undoubtedly true that events some people regard as miraculous are everyday occurrences to others. Take the birth of a baby for instance – a miracle to the baby's parents, but to a busy nurse part of her job and a normal everyday event. On the other hand, many people are still having experiences that nobody would hesitate to call 'miracles' in the traditional sense: dramatic, inexplicable, life-changing events. These are often attributed to guidance from the higher self, angelic or divine intervention.

At various points around the globe, shrines have been erected to visions of the Virgin Mary, Mejdugorje being one of the most impressive sites. The letters M I R (the Croatian for peace) are said to have appeared in the sky. Achill Island in County Mayo is another site of visions. The visions at these shrines, and many others, are said to be appearing to this day.

Glastonbury Thorn is a recurring miracle all may witness. The buds open on Christmas Day without fail. This hawthorn tree is claimed to have grown from the staff of Joseph of Arimathea. In 1582 Christmas was moved by several days with the introduction of the Gregorian Calendar, but the Thorn adapted and opened on Christmas Day as usual. Each Christmas a sprig is sent to the monarch.

HEALING MIRACLES

Many places of pilgrimage such as Lourdes in France are associated with miraculous cures. There are also a number of healers, some very famous, who claim to channel divine healing energy through their presence, prayers, or the laying on of hands. Cures may also happen through healing groups. There are also many instances of people spontaneously recovering from accidents and illness when doctors had given up on them, sometimes it seems with divine intervention. Here are some remarkable and inspiring healing stories.

The most moving stories I know are those involving children. Bethany's is no exception. The incident, which occurred when she was a young girl, had an emotional response from the whole community and I'm sure reverberates to this day even though Bethany is now adult. It happened when Bethany was seven years old, on a warm summer's evening in England. Bethany's father worked on a shift system and was preparing to leave. Bethany was to accompany him to the bus stop as usual and wave goodbye. The bus stop was on the opposite side of the road from Bethany's house so they crossed and waited for the bus to arrive.

The bus pulled up and, saying goodbye, Bethany's father stepped into the vehicle and took a seat. Before the bus pulled away, however, Bethany decided to dash across the road to her house, unable to see the car coming towards her, hidden by the stationary bus.

Vividly, she recalls the impact, the awful thud of the car coming into contact with her little frame, and how she was thrown into the air with the force of it, landing heavily on a grass verge. The next thing Bethany remembers is the experience of a very bright light, and a strong sense of being told to open her eyes. The light was helping her to be strong and she recalls no feelings of fear whatsoever. A family friend had lifted her in his arms and handed her to her mother who at this point was frantic with worry. Bethany was aware of all this and somehow secure in the knowledge that she would be perfectly all right, although her distraught mother and the neighbours all believed her to be dead.

In fact she sustained no serious injury. Later she told her mother that she believed Jesus had helped her open her eyes, obviously remembering all she had learned in Sunday school. One thing was clear, a modern-day miracle had occurred, because by all the laws of probability Bethany should not have survived such an impact.

Ilani is a talented athlete who shows great promise. You may be asking why that is so remarkable, for youngsters all over the country are skilled athletes, but they have not had Ilani's history. The very fact that she is a happy, healthy twelve-year-old is itself a miracle.

One day when she was six years old, Ilani's mother, Joanne, took her to join a small group of children and their mothers for a day in the park. Leaving the park, it was decided to go along together to the house of one of the group. Joanne left Ilani to walk with the group of children and adults and took her car, intending to call at her home for drinks and snacks to share.

It was a group brought together by the adults' interest in healing. Like so many healing groups, they believed that sending collective, concentrated distant healing brought powerful results.

Joanne found herself in a traffic jam. Sitting patiently for some time, she realized the best thing to do was park the car and walk. The distance was quite short and her feet would be faster at that point. To her horror, however, she discovered that the traffic congestion was due to Ilani having been hit by a car. She was lying unconscious and in need of an ambulance. Joanne later learned that the chattering group of children had reached the road ready to cross and Ilani had felt sure she had heard someone say it was all right to go ahead. The car was too close to avoid her and the little girl was struck.

The events of the next hour or so seemed unreal. The ambulance took Ilani to hospital, her father was found and driven there by a member of the group, and the whole group followed. On Ilani's arrival the team at the hospital swung into action and everything possible was done. X-rays were taken that revealed a broken hip. Joanne and her husband Steve asked the healing group to send healing to their little girl. Delighted to be able to contribute, they did their best.

It was obvious from the X-rays, however, that the paediatric consultant would be needed. Unfortunately, she was playing golf and the minutes seemed like hours until she was located. Eventually, she arrived at the hospital and, seeing Ilani's condition, insisted on additional X-rays being taken of a more comprehensive nature. These were then shown to the consultant who could scarcely believe her eyes. There were no broken bones at all. The doctor who had originally asked for X-rays was even more baffled. There could not possibly be a mistake, as Ilani was the only small girl admitted that day to casualty. The X-rays were clearly that of a small girl with a broken hip bone.

Ilani was in hospital for five days, badly bruised and shaken but nevertheless with bones intact. The healing group had concentrated as never before, and it seems that they brought about a miracle.

There is an elderberry bush outside my kitchen window, which in early summer is heavy with cream blossom and in autumn full of dark clumps of berries. For me it is special because it holds the memory of a day in spring spent with a dear friend, when all the odds had pointed to her never being able to see that day at all. I remember her smile and calmness as she told me the story of her own healing miracle.

Several years before she'd had very little to smile at for life was grim: a marriage containing little happiness, a series of illnesses and operations, culminating with the awful news being given to her: 'You have cancer, there is little we can do but treat you with drugs to make you more comfortable.' These words hit her like bricks hurled from a great height and she sat in her hospital bed long after the consultant had left, stunned and speechless. Slowly the shock left her, melting away until suddenly the inexplicable happened. She knew she was not going to die, a feeling of conviction deep inside defied all the facts.

To everyone's astonishment she refused all treatment offered and discharged herself the next day. At home, without any real insight into what she was doing, she sat calmly in an armchair, closed her eyes and visualized tiny cells with happy faces zipping through her body and killing the dark cancer cells. This is a visualization technique that has been used by many people, but she had not known this and was meditating almost automatically.

As time went by she began to feel better. Any contact from the hospital offering help or advice was calmly and politely refused. After six months the hospital asked her to come for a check-up, and this time she agreed. The consultant was happy to see her but puzzled by her appearance and demeanour. She was glowing and happy, positive that life had much in store for her. They checked, they tested, they X-rayed – and found she was completely clear of cancer. The astonishment was almost palpable as the consultant gazed at this woman. He knew spontaneous remission was not unheard of, but her attitude had taught him a great deal.

Many years down the track, sitting under my elderberry bush, I recall all the areas in life in which she has helped others: counselling in hospital, working with young people, helping with physical and spiritual healing. 'It's fairly obvious,' she said, 'why I was allowed my modern-day miracle and why I knew it was not my time to die.'

129

*

Gordon is a firm believer in miracles and the power of prayer and he feels truly blessed to be a recipient of a healing miracle. For some time, Gordon had had problems with his eyes, suffering from cataracts and glaucoma. He was supervised carefully and required to administer eyedrops several times daily.

The Swedenborgian Church in Sydney holds meetings for healing purposes, where angels are involved to help heal. Prayers were said for Gordon and his eye condition, and gradually the pressure decreased.

Ophthalmology is a very exact science, so the specialist taking care of Gordon was perplexed. He is of the Buddhist faith and a spiritual man, but had never witnessed such an inexplicable healing before. The eyedrops treatment is now minimal, and Gordon continues to improve, with ongoing gratitude for the healing meetings at which he was made so welcome.

ANGELIC AND DIVINE ENCOUNTERS

Researching my last book about people's experience of angel encounters, discovered that few were left with anything tangible to remind them of the event. There was such a variety of experiences, ranging from the touch of a hand to seeing a full-blown angel that I came to the conclusion that we see and feel what we can cope with. Here is a selection of stories involving angelic helpers and guidance from a supernatural or spiritual source.

Pauline states that she is a very practical person and would require a practical experience for her leap of faith. She did indeed receive a down-to-earth demonstration of angel power. I shall let her tell her own story.

'We were on holiday in the village of Upwey in Dorset. The cottage was beside the Upwey wishing well, an ancient well said to be a site of pagan worship, which attracts many people.

'About two days into the holiday, a crystal necklace which I always wear and never take off (it is an aqua-aura, a very spiritual stone) began to feel very tight around my neck whilst I was in bed and I felt that I had to take it off, which I did. I placed it on the table by the side of the bed and fell asleep. In the morning I reached out to put it back on but it wasn't there. I thought it must have fallen on to the floor and we searched under the bed and around the room but with no success. Being practical by nature I said it must be somewhere and it would turn up when we packed away our things to go home.

'During the next two weeks I kept checking for it but without any luck. On our last morning we packed everything away and checked every corner of the bedroom, but I was still unable to find the necklace. I stood in the bedroom and said, 'Please return my crystal because I am very fond of it and it helps in my healing work.' We were just about to leave when my husband John said he would have one last look around the room. He suddenly pointed to the opposite corner of the room where the bed was. In this corner was a table, on which was my crystal. Placed next to the crystal was a large white feather. Neither had been there earlier! As I picked up the feather I got goose pimples from head to toe and immediately my intuition told me that it was a feather from an angel's wing and it had been left to prove to me that my angel helper is always there and I must have faith. My crystal was immediately fastened around my neck and I felt wonderful. Other people have held the feather and all have had a similar sensation to mine. It also seems to help with healing if I draw it through the person's aura. I feel it was a wonderful gift.'

Trains and railway stations link our next stories. One story is told by John Ronner in *The Angels of Cokeville*. It took place in England where a young woman was taking a train to Cambridge where her fiancé would be waiting to meet her.

At every station where the train stopped, to the young girl's amazement, a ghostly double of her fiancé gestured to her to get off the train. Finally, at one station, the figure was gesturing so wildly and had such a terrified look on its face that the girl felt compelled to leave the train. Soon afterwards the train crashed and the coach she had been in was demolished.

During all this time, her fiancé was asleep in the waiting room at Cambridge and was not even aware of dreaming.

Sydney, Australia, is the venue for the following events, again at a railway station. A woman was to take a late train from the station to travel to the country. She was rather nervous, knowing of several incidents where muggings had taken place in that particular area. As she approached the station, an older man came up and spoke to her, voicing his concern and offering to escort her on to the platform in safety. They walked through the area which had caused her alarm and reached the station safely. Escorting her on to the platform, the man assured her she was now safe. Turning to thank him, she found he had vanished. There was absolutely nowhere he could have gone in that moment. In utter amazement she simply caught the train.

By added coincidence, her son was also involved in an incident late at night whilst travelling on a train. The young man was a nursing aide and had finished a late shift at the hospital. He noticed a crowd of unsavoury-looking characters climb aboard. The gang were carrying spray cans and were obviously about to cause damage to the train and anyone who tried to prevent them. It was difficult not to feel nervous as they came down the carriage towards him. They said the police were patrolling the train and would he please hide their spray cans in his case. They told him that he personally was in no danger because of the huge companion obviously protecting him. Stunned, he looked from their faces to the seat next to him, following their respectful gaze – the seat was empty!

Melany works as a researcher in radio, a job she loves. The only occasional problem is working late at night. It was past midnight one night when she started the car and left the radio station. Her journey at a certain point necessitated driving through none too salubrious an area. Arriving at a certain point on a deserted stretch of road, Melany saw to her horror a dog lying in her path. She was most distressed and stopped the car. Without thinking, she leapt from the vehicle and ran to the dog, which was dead, but she could not leave it there in the middle of the road. The least she ought to do was place it at the kerb, but she realized she could not touch it.

Crying softly at this point, she was suddenly aware of just how vulnerable she was. The road had few buildings, and the ones in evidence appeared to be derelict. There had been no other traffic whilst she stood there and she was quite at a loss as to what she should do next. To her alarm, she felt a hand on her shoulder and turned to see an exceptionally tall young man. At this point, Melany was shaking with fright and wishing she had stayed in her car. He spoke with a soft, calm, reassuring voice, however. 'Please don't be afraid. Go back to your car and I'll deal with this little dog.' Thankfully, Melany slipped back into the driving seat and locked her door, although by now all the fear had left her.

The young man lifted the dog gently and placed it on the small grass verge at the kerb side. He then started to walk directly down the road in the direction Melany had come from. She breathed a sigh of relief, started the engine and looked in the rear-view mirror wanting to hoot her horn in thanks and goodbye.

Glancing in the mirror, however, she discovered the young man was nowhere to be seen. He had literally vanished into thin air in the few seconds between him walking past the car and Melany looking in her rear-view mirror. If the dog had not been on the grass verge she would have been tempted to think she had imagined it all. It was real though, and Melany still thinks of it as her own mini-miracle.

Anyone who has spent time in a desert will tell you what an inhospitable environment it is. One has to be well prepared, even when driving through on a well-kept road. Water, food and emergency equipment are essential in event of an accident or breakdown. Since by day the temperatures can be in excess of 30 degrees and by night below freezing, my next story is all the more remarkable.

It happened in Arizona when a little girl had been abducted, snatched from her suburban garden. The vehicle left the highway and went deep into desert territory before pushing the little girl out of the car and leaving her confused and crying, miles away from anywhere. She had up to this point been unharmed and the reason for the abduction remains a mystery. The frightening point was that here, with no food or water, and without suitable clothing, was a five-year-old girl, totally alone in the desert.

Four days and nights passed. Her frantic family and all the emergency services feared the worst. On the fourth day, the police received a call from a man out hunting. He had found a little girl by the main desert highway, safe, well and cheerful.

Reunited with her family, she was questioned. They could scarcely believe she had survived all that time in the desert, for an adult would certainly have died. She replied that she had been most happy because another child had looked after her. She had been dressed in white with blue eyes and surrounded by a bright shining light. This child had led her to the highway where she was found unscathed.

Beth and Michael were great walkers. One year they

took a spring holiday in America, staying in Santa
Barbara, and decided to go walking in the Sierra
Nevada mountains. They were sensibly dressed and
equipped, and hoped to reach a high point to view as
much of the surrounding area as possible. After several
hours they reached the snow line, surprised at not
having seen another living soul, even though it was not
a traditional holiday time or a weekend.

Deciding at mid-afternoon that it was time to
retrace their steps they turned back and followed the
route they had come. It looked unfamiliar and reaching a fork they were perplexed, for they had no recol-
lection of the path dividing as they had climbed up.
Poring over the map did not help and a fear that they
might be lost started to enter their heads. Choosing
one path they walked a little way but thought it was a
good deal steeper than they remembered, full of rocks
which were snow-covered and made walking quite difficult. At this point Michael lost his footing and fell
quite heavily, missing a steep gully by a very narrow
margin. There was a large cut on the back of his head
and he felt dazed and dizzy. Beth was by now fighting
panic, but she coped with the wound, placing a large
plaster over it, and Michael struggled to get to his feet.

Suddenly there was a figure standing right behind
them. Beth was astonished for she had not seen him
approach and the path was so exposed. Even more
extraordinary, the man was not wearing a jacket; only

a black sweater and trousers. Smiling at her, he bent down and lifted Michael to his feet with tremendous ease – a great feat with a tall and heavy man. Michael felt a surge of heat through his body and his strength returned. The man told them they must go back a short distance and take the other path and all would be well. He walked ahead of them until they were safely on the right track and wished them well.

They thanked him profusely and set off, pausing to turn and wave, only to find he had vanished! There was nowhere he could have gone to – no turns on the path, no trees – and they had only moved a few yards any-way. Stunned, they looked at each other; then Michael looked down at the ground. They could clearly see the point where they had left the man and in the snow there were only two sets of footprints, one very large set of boot prints that were Michael's and a small set of Beth's prints. They looked in all directions but the man was nowhere to be seen.

Arriving safely at the car Michael insisted he was well enough to drive, in fact, he felt full of strength and energy. Totally amazed by the incident they drove away and Beth said, 'If anyone ever witnessed a miracle it was me.'

Kyle Benetz was a happy two-year-old boy living in Philadelphia when he was diagnosed as suffering from a brain tumour. This was the start of several traumatic years for the little boy and his devastated parents. The tumour was in the worst possible position and the initial surgery only removed one third of it. Kyle's parents were facing the fact that their son might die and it felt as though they were living in a nightmare. Chemotherapy was used but the tumour continued to grow. The optic nerve became involved and the prognosis became worse than ever.

Further surgery was not recommended, as this might reduce Kyle to a vegetative state. However, his parents, Connie and Dave, had a strong faith and due to exposure of their plight in a magazine found themselves receiving many letters, many mentioning a surgeon in another state named Dr Wisoff. What was to be done? Should they stop the treatment and perhaps cause their son to die – or seek help elsewhere in the hope that the advice was sound? There were all sorts of complications in obtaining a consultation with Dr Wisoff, not least that he practised in another state (New York).

Connie could not sleep, caught as she was between a rock and a hard place. She felt deep down inside that the most positive thing she could do was pray and enlist the prayers of others. She printed a letter saying they planned to opt for further surgery at the hands of this remarkable man, the decision was difficult, but would as many people as possible please pray for Kyle. The letters were delivered to Kyle's school and to over a hundred churches and synagogues.

Soon afterwards, Connie was in her kitchen washing dishes, Kyle was asleep and the house empty and quiet save for the two of them. In tears, Connie silently prayed to be given strength to face the days ahead. Next, she began to feel the atmosphere change. The room was filled with light and a presence she guessed to be an angel was there with her.

Suddenly a musical box started playing unaided the tune 'Amazing Grace', beginning at the very first note and continuing precisely to the last. It was an angel musical box. Connie stared in disbelief, but she knew in her heart that God was speaking to her and the message was: keep going, keep fighting, you're not alone. As a result, Kyle was taken to New York and placed in the care of Dr Wisoff.

Today, aged nine, Kyle attends school, a happy, healthy, normal child. This simple everyday event is one they thought they would never see but, here they are, grateful for the surgeon's skills, for their son's courage, the support of others, their faith in God – and Connie's very special miracle.

LISTEN TO YOUR INNER VOICE

Many of us have had the experience of a premonition or an 'inner voice' that comes from nowhere but proves to be extremely significant. Kevin has had such experiences on more than one occasion.

Kevin was driving to meet his father, aware that he was late. He did not want his father to be standing waiting and so put his foot down on the accelerator, knowing this was not a good idea. Apart from breaking the speed limit, he was a very new driver and not really confident enough to handle the car at speed. Glancing down, he saw that he was travelling at 70 mph. A voice came from nowhere and said, 'What if you have an accident at 70 mph?' This made him react instantly and take his foot off the accelerator, and he breathed a sigh of relief as the car slowed. Whilst he was making his way through the lanes of traffic to the inside lane, there was a loud bang, and Kevin, fighting for control, realized a rear tyre had blown. Breaking out in a cold sweat, he safely brought the car to a standstill. Shaking, he thought of the very different result there would have been had he continued at 70 mph. Silently, he thanked the voice.

Having experienced this warning voice once, Kevin was even swifter to react on the second occasion. He was on the top rung of a pair of stepladders, held together by a piece of string. They were old and, as he balanced precariously on the top, he heard the voice say a second time, 'What if you should have an accident at the top of these ladders?' Kevin immediately but carefully climbed down. When he was almost at the bottom the string snapped. He jumped safely to the floor, only seconds before the ladders collapsed.

In parapsychology, the hearing of 'inner' sounds or voices is called clairaudience (French for 'clear hearing'). Many people in all walks of life have heard these voices. It has happened several times to Peter in his ministry and he never ignores it, knowing for certain he is needed.

Peter was a busy minister, and fairly new to his church, so on a free afternoon he decided some pastoral visiting would be both useful and pleasurable. Setting off with no particular person in mind he drove in the direction of some of his far-flung flock. At this point, forcefully and with great clarity but totally unprompted, a name came into Peter's head. It remained fixed in his consciousness so he felt he had no other choice than to visit this woman, even though it would mean a drive of well over an hour.

The woman had been to church and Peter had talked to her but he had met her husband only briefly. Arriving at the house he was met at the door by the husband, clearly in a highly emotional state. A full twenty minutes elapsed before Peter could calm him sufficiently to elicit his problem. A short time ago, possibly the exact moment her name had entered Peter's head, she had died, and had just been taken in an ambulance to hospital. If ever anyone was needed at that time it was Peter, whose chief area of interest was bereavement counselling.

Here is another example of Peter's clairaudience. Again driving to a house named by his inner voice, he reached the avenue to see the family dog running down the centre of the road. This was extremely unusual, for the dog was well controlled and would not normally be allowed to wander. Stopping his car, Peter noticed the garden gate and the front door were wide open. He knew at once something was amiss. Announcing himself, he quickly walked into the lounge where he found the wife sobbing and distressed. Her husband had just died. Yet again, Peter was urgently needed and could give all the help and comfort his counselling skills had prepared him for.

Jo is someone who feels sure she is guided. This is her story, in her own words.

'I have always lived by my instincts and intuition, frequently keeping these feelings to myself for fear of being laughed at. Sometimes it feels like a gentle nudge from above but occasionally it's a warning, to be ignored at my peril. This was certainly the case the last time I felt a warning instinctively. But what was I being warned about? I had no idea. My unease felt even more incongruous on such a wonderful summer's day.

'My husband and I set off for our usual weekly shopping trip. I tried hard to ignore my inner voice and disquiet. Suddenly I knew I must ignore this no longer and turning to my husband said, "Please drive with extra care and as slowly as possible, I fear we may be involved in an accident." Most men would have felt insulted if they, like my husband, held advanced driving qualifications and were ex-policemen. However, experience of my intuition has taught him not to be sceptical, and he duly slowed down.

'Shopping completed, we chose to drive home the scenic way, as it was such glorious weather and the major roads were sure to fall victim to snarl-ups. In a country lane we came across a group of youngsters on bicycles. My husband slowed and cautiously drove past them. The lane narrowed at this point and the children, not terribly attentive, were giggling and, one boy in particular, wobbling erratically. Suddenly this boy pulled out wide into the road just as we were passing the group and collided with the passenger side of the car. Horrified, I watched it all unfolding as if in slow motion. Bouncing off the car he then crashed into the roadside wall and hit the ground hard.

'Quickly stopping the car we ran back to pick him up and were relieved to find him shaken but only suffering from sore knees and elbows. His friends gave us directions to the boy's home and we delivered him safely to his mother.

'We were also badly shaken, but passing the accident spot once more we realized he had bounced off a deflector post, positioned to prevent cars hitting the wall at night. We were flooded with a sense of gratitude not to have been going any faster, for he certainly would have been under the front wheels of the car. Had I received a warning? Was it simply a coincidence? Only you can decide, but I know what I believe.'

You could hardly think of a more mundane item than a five-pound note. We pause to think only briefly about them when making a purchase or musing on how quickly they disappear from our wallets when shopping. The five-pound note, however, takes on a more significant and meaningful role in the next story and represents a dilemma many of us have faced at one time or another.

It was a miserable day in the city, grey and grisly with a cold that seeped through even the warmest winter clothing. Daniel was reaching the end of his shopping trip. It was growing dark as he hurried down a side street to his last port of call, an art shop. He had left a painting to be framed some time ago and it was ready for collection. Mercifully, it had already been paid for because at this point Daniel realized he had only a £5 note and a 50p coin and most of that would be taken in his train-fare home.

Suddenly, out of a doorway, a bedraggled figure stepped into his path. 'Have you any money to spare?' was the request. Daniel looked at him, possibly the same age as himself, mid-twenties but, tired, wet, dishevelled and hungry, he looked much older. Daniel paused momentarily. This man was in obvious need and 50p would seem useless, but if he gave him the £5 how would he get home? Having weighed this up almost instantly, Daniel pulled out the £5 and gave it to the young man. The look on his face was enough to convince Daniel he'd done the right thing. 'God bless you,' said the young man. Daniel hurried on to catch the shop before closing, pondering on what to do next. He could travel in the bus as far as 50p would take him and walk the rest of the way home, five miles at least he calculated.

Reaching the art shop, he was relieved to see it was still open. Pushing the door, he glanced down to see a £5 note on the doormat, wet but intact. Amazed, he picked it up and went into the shop, collected his picture and asked if anyone had enquired about a lost £5. 'No,' said the shopkeeper, 'people often have no idea where they drop their money and I'm closing now. You keep it, sir, I'm sure it's meant for you.' God had blessed him, thought Daniel.

ANIMAL POWER

In 1982 an extraordinary event happened in Seattle, Washington State, at around midnight. A paramedic and his partner were called to attend an accident. A vehicle had apparently careered over the edge of a cliff, but the paramedics could make out nothing in the dark. One paramedic shone a bright light down the ravine where he saw to his surprise a golden retriever climbing towards him, who obviously wanted the paramedic to follow him. Carefully, he followed the dog down the ravine, where he found the wreck.

The paramedic radioed for help and finally the badly injured motorist was rescued. The dog was nowhere to be seen at this point. In the excitement it must have disappeared. A few minutes later, a firefighter happened to state in the hearing of the paramedic that there was just one person in the car, and of course the dog. The paramedic stared into the rear of the car. Sprawled on the back seat was a golden retriever that had been crushed and killed instantly on impact. The paramedic shivered.

If you will pardon the pun, this is the tale of a cat called Molly. The Burton family adored Molly. She had been part of their family since kittenhood and was particularly close to the two little girls who told Molly all their secrets, knowing they would go no further. The family lived in a spacious top-floor flat with lovely views across the fields and a small wood. When going on holiday they would all scramble into the family caravan, Molly peeping out of the window, riding in style and enjoying the holiday as much as anyone.

One year, however, it was decided to take a holiday in Italy. The problem of Molly, however, was acute. No-one could bear to put her into a cat hostel, the neighbours were not very keen to take care of her, and everyone started to worry. Grandma Burton had the solution: she would take care of Molly. So they put her in a basket and drove her to her holiday with Grandma. It was a fifteen-mile drive, and Molly, shut in the cat basket on the rear seat of the car, complained loudly all the way. The girls cried as they said goodbye to her but their father laughed, telling them she would be back with them in two weeks' time.

The holiday was a great success, and the girls did not want to return home, but the thought of seeing Molly again cheered them as they made their way to the airport. As the plane touched down, all the girls could think about was collecting their beloved Molly. It was becoming increasingly obvious to their parents that calling home first to drop off luggage was completely out of the question, so, bowing to the inevitable, they went straight to Grandma's house.

Excited knocking brought Grandma to the door but instead of the usual beaming smile, she looked crestfallen and tearful. 'Whatever's wrong?' they asked and Grandma had to confess that Molly was missing. Disoriented and pining she had run off one morning almost a week ago and had not been seen since.

Grandma had searched, her friends and neighbours had searched, the local animal welfare group had searched, but all to no avail; Molly had gone. The girls were quite inconsolable and poor Grandma was greatly distressed. Eventually, however, they had to accept that their cherished Molly was lost.

Gloomily, they drove home, parked the car and took the lift with their heavy suitcases to the top floor. At the front door, the girls' mother reached in her handbag for the keys but she froze in the act, for there sitting in front of the door was Molly! The joy and excitement that followed would be hard to describe, but eventually the woman from the flat below appeared and said Molly had turned up about four days ago and refused to move from the flat door, so she fed her and gave her drinks until the family came home. The mystery is that Molly had arrived home after walking fifteen miles, from a house she had been taken to locked inside a dark cat basket, crossing a busy motorway and a river on the way. One thing seems certain, love had been the spur.

Beatrix Potter must have imbued countless numbers of children with a love of rabbits. We take toy ones to bed, decorate children's bedrooms and clothes with them and attribute human qualities to them. There are those amongst us, it has to be said, who grow less fond of these furry friends with passing years, chiefly when our children who swear to love and take care of the rabbit, then lose all interest and dirty cages become the parent's lot. Karen falls into this category, not by any means an animal person, but tolerating them for her children's sake. This makes her story all the more puzzling.

It was Christmastime and Karen was staying with relatives in Belfast. On a shopping trip with her sister and sister-in-law, she suddenly saw a pet store. On impulse, she decided to buy her nephew a goldfish to accompany the lone one he had recently acquired. As they entered the pet store, she saw an enormous black lop-eared rabbit staring plaintively from its cage. Karen was totally captivated. She approached the cage and the rabbit raised its paws up to the bars and stared into her eyes. It seemed almost human and she wanted to buy it more than any animal she had ever seen. Totally out of character, she was quite besotted by the rabbit.

However, since they had to fly home to Manchester after the Christmas holidays it was impossible to take the rabbit on the plane. Karen could think of nothing else. The lovely face seemed to haunt her and she really could not understand why it seemed so important that she should own this rabbit.

Christmas passed happily enough and Karen flew back to England with her family. Arriving home in a bustle of suitcases and belongings, she put on the kettle for a cup of tea. She had a sudden impulse to check their own rabbit which was being cared for by a friend during the holiday. The friend looked crestfallen and told her the pet was dead. All sorts of thoughts, feelings and symbolism filled her head. What did it all mean?

The next story concerns the miraculous safe-keeping of treasured objects. It begins in 1850 in the north of England, in a place called Northwich in the county of Cheshire, as a young man called James Ridgeway sets off for a new life in South Africa. James belonged to the church whose spiritual beliefs are based on the writings of Emanuel Swedenborg, so a complete set of these writings was a highly prized possession which James placed in a trunk for the voyage. Many other important papers and documents were also packed in this trunk for the journey.

Arriving eventually in Durban, James and his wife found a cottage for rent not far from the river-bank. Unknown hazards were lurking, however, for shortly after settling in there was a great flooding of the river. Breaking free from the confines of the river gorge, it rose and flooded the whole area, rapidly gaining in strength and becoming an extremely dangerous flash-flood.

The cottage was in imminent danger of being washed away completely and the couple thought that was what was going to happen, when, to their relief, the waters stopped just three feet from the door. People and belongings were safe, including the documents and writings so precious and close to James's heart.

They soon realized that, although they were safe for the moment, the river would always present a danger and so the only course of action was to move to somewhere safer. On arrival at their new home, however, their relief turned to dismay, for on opening the stout trunk, they discovered that all the papers were being eaten by termites. As he lifted the mangled papers from the trunk, James was filled with despair, until he reached the set of books by Swedenborg. They were perfectly intact, whilst all the other papers had been destroyed.

RELIGIOUS MIRACLES

Undoubtedly many people still think of miracles in association with religious events and experiences and indeed, even in modern times, there are many miraculous incidents that seem to be brought about through the power of religious faith. I would like to end this book with a few particularly inspiring examples.

Picture Galilee, say the word to yourself, and your mind will probably be flooded with biblical images of fishing boats and hot sun. Ann knew that this place would contain special meaning for her.

The greatest sadness of the year had been the death of Ann's mother. She felt quite bereft, but more than that she sought some form of comfort and assurance that death was not the end. Ann's mother had been a Christian with a firm belief in life after death. She was convinced they would be together again, but Ann was full of uncertainties and questions. Struggling as she was at this point, a holiday in Israel sounded ideal and her husband was most supportive and encouraged her to go.

The holiday included a visit to Galilee. Ann alighted from the coach which had stopped by the sea shore. The magic and history of that location was almost palpable. The original plan was that the party would sail across the lake to Tiberius, but the sea was decidedly choppy and growing more so by the minute. The boats they were to sail in were built in the ancient style, not very robust, though with engines. They were faced with a decision of whether to brave the rough waters or ride around the lake in the coach to Tiberius. Ann chose the boat. She felt compelled to sail on the sea Jesus had sailed almost two thousand years before and she wasn't going to pass up the opportunity. Most people opted to ride and the coach set off down the road.

The brave ones took to the water and even the

boat's owner admitted that the sea was not usually this rough though squalls were not unknown. Powering through the waves they reached a point some two-thirds of the way across. The boat owner, who declared himself to be a Christian, suddenly stopped the boat. He said it was his custom to stop to allow people to absorb the atmosphere and indeed Ann was beginning to feel a spiritually moving sensation.

There was silence on the little boat as it pitched and tossed, and then someone suggested they said a prayer. Everyone readily agreed and bowed their heads for a simple, moving prayer. Ann felt very emotional and close to tears, feeling her mother's presence for the first time and fully understanding what her mother's faith had meant. The vacation and the atmosphere were affecting her greatly and she felt strongly the urge to be involved in some other form of worship, to give thanks on a personal level for her spiritual uplifting. Tentatively, she suggested singing a hymn and to her delight everyone readily agreed. They found a hymn with a tune everyone knew and started to sing *Dear Lord and Father of Mankind*.

They were half-way through this hymn when in an instant the sea became calm. Swift storm and calm are not unknown in this region, but even the boat's owner admitted he had never experienced a change so swiftly before. Slowly, they made their way to the shore and arrived at Tiberius in virtual silence, everyone lost in their own thoughts about the incident. Ann felt certain at last that death was not the end and also felt a calm that mirrored the Sea of Galilee.

They disembarked, and related the story to their waiting friends. The boat's owner finished the story by saying that although there was really no way he knew for certain, he always stopped his boat at roughly the same spot, for as a Christian it was very meaningful for him. It was generally believed in that area that it was the spot where Jesus had calmed the storm. Ann now feels that day was a real turning point in her life.

One modern-day miracle happened during a seminar for Reform Rabbis. A meditation was being led by Rabbi Lionel Blue. The meditators sat in a circle and placed a candle in the centre. For unknown reasons the candle would not light even after several attempts, and the wick had burned down into the hollow. Lionel Blue said they would just have to imagine the flame. After the meditation, one person stated that he had been very upset that the candle would not light, since it signified an event in his own life, which had caused him to lose confidence. During meditation he had been unable to think of anything else. He tried eventually to light it again, simultaneously trying to rekindle his inner spirit, but had grown more and more despondent.

Rabbi Jonathan Romain, who related this story, says that at this point he gave a start, for the candle was flickering and within moments had become a steady flame. Everyone was convinced that no-one had lit the candle, yet it glowed its message for all to see.

The next story is set in the days before Christmas, the first Christmas of peace after the Second World War, when miracles would have been especially welcome.

Everyone wanted to ensure that this would be a very special Christmas. In London's East End, the vicar of St Leonard's was pondering on how best he could brighten up his church for the festival. Three years previously, a German bomb had blasted out the east window behind the altar. Since that day the window had been boarded up, with the result that the altar looked very shabby. The vicar was at a loss as to what he could do. Curtaining in a rich fabric might help, but its availability was questionable. One thing was certain, the boarding would have to be disguised to make the church more welcoming for Christmas.

The vicar decided to visit the local market to see if there was anything at all suitable. He walked the length and breadth of the market, checking every stall, but nothing emerged that he felt would be right. On the very last stall, his eye fell on a bundle of second-hand velvet, and he asked the stall holder how much the bundle would be. 'Well, mate,' said the stall holder, 'I haven't really had the time to open it up and see what's there. Give me a pound and take the bundle.' Full of hope, the vicar paid up, put the bundle into his car and drove home.

When he opened the bundle at home he was delighted and astonished to find he had a great bargain. Unrolling the swathe of rich red velvet, he discovered the centre was exquisitely embroidered with a Nativity scene of the stable with the shepherds and three wise men paying tribute to the Holy Family.

The cloth was carefully pressed by the vicar's wife and hung in place behind the altar, where it looked beautiful. The vicar hurried back to the market stall holder to press him into accepting some extra money, but the stall holder would have none of it. 'Please accept it as a Christmas gift for the church,' he said. The vicar was delighted and thanked him profusely for his kindness.

On Christmas Eve, the vicar thought he would like to take one more look at the artistry. As he turned to leave, he heard the sound of sobbing and saw a woman kneeling in a pew, tears streaming down her face. 'Whatever is the matter?' the vicar asked. 'If I can do anything to help I will gladly do so.' The woman, calming a little, replied, 'I am a refugee from Belgium. My husband and I fled from the Germans.' The vicar waited patiently as she composed herself. 'We were separated in the confusion and he was captured and killed,' she explained. 'Today I have travelled right across London answering an advertisement for a job. I didn't get it and felt so low I came into your church to pray.'

She continued talking and the vicar listened. At home in Belgium she had lived in a large house and in the hall she had hung a piece of embroidery very similar to the one behind the altar. 'Come and look more closely,' said the vicar. 'It's a beautiful piece of work.' As she came nearer the idea that it might conceivably be hers flitted through her mind. 'I embroidered my initials, E. S., in one corner,' she said. They went right up to the cloth and examined it closely. Sure enough, in one corner were the initials, E. S., barely noticeable. Overjoyed, the lady declared she was mystified as to how it had arrived in London, but delighted it had found a good home. The vicar felt sure that with such skills a job would be found and he would be happy to help. 'Let me have your name and address and I'll make some inquiries,' he said.

On Christmas morning, the vicar was out of bed early and arrived at church for the special service, which went very well. After the service the vicar noticed one of the congregation lingering behind in the chancel. The man wished him a happy Christmas. They started to chat and the man said he was fascinated by the Nativity embroidery. He told the vicar he had lived in Bruges, where before the war he and his wife had a large house. His wife was most talented and had embroidered a cloth almost a replica of the one in the church, which had hung in their hall and been much admired. When the Germans arrived, they had fled in only the clothes they were wearing, with no time for any other belongings to be packed. He added that he and his wife had been separated in the confusion and he had heard she had died. 'This embroidery moves me greatly,' he said, the precious memories flooding back.

The vicar beamed at him, 'Your wife is not dead. This is her work and I know where she lives. Get into my car and I'll take you.' That Christmas morning two people, each believing the other to be dead, were reunited. They received the best Christmas present of their lives.

For me, coincidences are evidence of a powerful spiritual connection threading together people and time and guiding us to view our lives holistically, as part of the very web of life. The more we start to notice the many synchronicities and coincidences in our lives, the more complete the picture will become. The true pattern of our life will emerge, and with it the reality of God's influence. There will be a spiritual level at which we are all touched by divine order.

When we experience a coincidence, even at a very mundane level, this can serve as an expansion of our awareness, a glimpse into another dimension. Out of the blue, we may have glimpses of heaven . . .

If you have had an angel experience and wish to share it with the author, please contact her care of Rider Books, Editorial Department, Random House, 20 Vauxhall Bridge Road, London SW1V 2SA, or email her at glennyceeckersley@hotmail.com

Further Reading

Coincidence

Anderson, Ken, *Coincidence* (Blandford, 1995)

Harrison, P. and M. *Mystic Forces* (Sinclair, 1989)

Inglis, Brian, *Coincidence* (Hutchinson, 1990)

Jung, Carl, *Synchronicity* (ARK, 1995)

Koestler, Arthur, *The Roots of Coincidence* (Hutchinson, 1972)

Peat, David F., *Synchronicity* (Bantam, 1988)

Ronner, John, *The Angels of Cokeville* (Mamre, 1995)

Von Franz, M. L., *On Divination and Synchronicity* (Inner City, 1980)

Chaos

Briggs, John, *Fractals* (Thames & Hudson, 1992)

Gleick, James, *Chaos* (Abacus, 1993)

Psychology/Theology

Jung, Carl, *Man and His Symbols* (Picador, 1978)

Swedenborg, Emanuel, *Arcana Caelestia* (Swedish Society, 1983)

—, *Divine Providence* (Swedish Society, 1949)

Tribal Wisdom

Bates, Brian, *Wisdom of the Wyrd* (Rider, 1996)

Herbert, Marie, *Healing Quest* (Rider, 1996)

Morgan, Marlo, *Mutant Message Down Under* (Thorsons, 1994)

Peat, David F., *Blackfoot Physics* (Fourth Estate, 1995)

Mike Rowland's tapes are available from:

New World Cassettes, Wenhaston, Halesworth, Suffolk IP19 8RH

If you have enjoyed *Angels and Miracles*, you will also want to read Glennyce Eckersley's *An Angel At My Shoulder* . . .

'This book touches the soul and opens the door to the realm where heaven and earth meet and love abounds'

Denise Linn, author of *Sacred Space*

An Angel At My Shoulder shows angels are returning – and being acknowledged – once again. Here are true stories of countless ordinary people being rescued by angels, being comforted and healed by them, feeling their presence in the face of death – and often appearing to little children. These tales are drawn from such countries as Britain, Australia, Ireland and the United States – showing angels can be found all round the globe: helping people, often changing their lives completely.

As well as *Children and Angels*:

In this wonderful book, the author shows how children experience angels in many different forms – in traditional guise, with wings; as a simple light or fragrance; as heavenly voices and music – or as people in modern-day clothing.

Full of extraordinary, true stories from all round the globe, *Children and Angels* is an enchanting book that will open your eyes to new possibilities, and to other worlds.